*Books by Patricia Hart McMillan
and Rose Bennett Gilbert:*

DECORATING COUNTRY-STYLE: THE LOOK AND HOW TO HAVE IT

THE YOU-DO-IT BOOK OF EARLY AMERICAN DECORATING

Decorating
Country-style

Decorating

THE LOOK AND

Patricia Hart McMillan

1980

Country-style

HOW TO HAVE IT

and Rose Bennett Gilbert

DOUBLEDAY & COMPANY, INC., GARDEN CITY, NEW YORK

With special thanks to

Evan Francis, editor-in-chief, *1,001 Decorating Ideas*, and to
the magazine for photographs of Pat McMillan's home,
and to Hilda Sachs, New York Home Fashions publicist.

Illustrations by Ray Skibinski

Library of Congress Cataloging in Publication Data
McMillan, Patricia Hart.
    Decorating country-style.
    Includes index.
    1. Interior decoration.   2. Decoration and ornament, Rustic.   I. Gilbert, Rose Bennett, joint
author.   II. Title.
NK1986.R8M3   747'.8'83

ISBN: 0-385-14086-X
Library of Congress Catalog Card Number 78–68324

To my husband, George,
my son, George III,
and my daughters,
Elizabeth, Katharine, and Leigh.

For my sons, Scott and Bennett Gilbert,
because they never developed sibling rivalry
with my typewriter.

Cornering Country in a bedroom corner: The collector who lives here has tin treasures gleaned from country stores your great-grandfather would have known how to shop. Designer Ray Kindell has grouped the old canisters so they make a charming decorating statement against an appropriately old-fashioned background of fringed draperies, hung strap-style from a painted wooden pole.

Contents

Coming Home to Down-home Decorating

It is an early morning in the fall, the kind of morning when the cows' breath steams like the milk in the buckets Jean-Claude stands watching his working man carry in from the barn. Ordinarily, Jean-Claude himself would be still behind the drawn curtains of his *lit clos*, his closed-off bed, where he is safe from night vapors and chilling draughts. But this morning he woke in a strange bed, alone, down the hallway from the room where his wife and their new daughter were still sleeping.

It is the year 1755, Louis XV is reigning over France, Pompeii and Herculaneum have been discovered and will soon dominate the imaginations of the King and his court, along with the rest of civilized Europe. But Jean-Claude doesn't know about Pompeii yet—the news moves in lazy concentric ripples out from Paris to the provinces—and even if he did, today there's something special on his mind. As soon as the man returns from stowing the milk, they will go to cut down the large cherry tree out behind the kitchen garden. The wood will be stacked carefully in the highest part of the barn to season slowly through the years while the tiny daughter who arrived only last night is growing into womanhood. When she does, when it is time for her to be betrothed and married, then Jean-Claude will have that wood brought down from the barn, mellow and sweet from its years of waiting, and the best cabinetmaker within reach, old Jacques-Louis (or maybe Jacques' son by then), will carve it into a magnificent bed and a towering armoire. They will be for her dower, a part of her heritage literally rooted in her family soil . . . much, much more than merely household furnishings. . . .

We hope you're reading this on a subway somewhere. Or maybe standing in the aisle of a modern bookstore, being jostled by passersby. You've had to check all your shopping bags at the door, and you will pay for your choices with a plastic card full of embossed numbers. Or, perhaps instead, you're sitting within your own four walls: square, spare; right angles everywhere; window, a vast hole in the wall that stares, unblinking, across a city street or into a neighbor's driveway.

Because, if your environment's anything like most Americans' today as we hurtle toward the end of the twentieth century, leaving scraps and shreds of former values and traditions and treasures littering the way behind us like burned-out power modules in space, then the story of Jean-Claude and his daughter's furniture is giving you a twinge of envy.

The twinge is a surface symptom of a marrow-deep disorder diagnosed variously as rootlessness, as loss of continuity, as rebellion against impending impersonality. If this is indeed a malady of the times, then the eyes have it, too. Enough of the hard-edged and surface-brilliant. Enough of less being more and of being reduced to numbers, and enough of the Bureau of Standards as an arbiter of taste.

After nearly a century of the slick, the standardized and the sterile, our psyches, our aesthetics, and our imaginations are all protesting in one voice. The tune we're singing is "Bring back the good old days." Bring back materials we can touch and trust: wood, stone, marble, cane, and wicker, and homespun fabrics of linen and wool and cotton. In short, bring back the earth and the fullness thereof. Bring back the *ambiance* of those other earlier days when porch-sitting was high entertainment, when there was the time for needlepoint and patchwork, when home represented a family haven, and furniture, like aging relatives, was treasured for itself and not expected to be trendy.

Is this longing for yesteryear, so obviously expressed in our homes and our clothes, really a wish for a *return* to other times? Or is it more of an *arrival*, an arrival at new levels of appreciation for human-ness, for simplicity, for individuality? After two-hundred-plus years of growth, of melding, of working toward a common image for all Americans, we are now ready to get back to our individual heritages. Pausing in mid-step after centuries of head-

Here's true home-style heirloom collecting: The heirlooms are homes. The urge back to country living inspired a North Carolina couple to collect the log cabin a great-great-uncle built back in 1896 and move it down country roads to their own backyard. The restored cabin, left, is filled with furnishings handed down through the family. Another North Carolina man spent America's Bicentennial Year rechinking the logs and relaying the fieldstone chimney on the log cabin his father had built in 1904, above. All over the country, old buildings with historic or just plain sentimental value are being nurtured back to life as we seek to get in touch with our beginnings.

long growth when bigger *was* better, when *more* was the goal, we're now evaluating our next direction. We're researching our motives and re-evaluating our goals, both as a nation and as individuals. Historians could say "I told you so." Civilization has always resisted overrefinement. Down through the centuries, the world seems to have righted itself, to have gotten back in touch with reality, just when it looked most likely to spin completely off in uncharted directions. Sometimes the means seemed to signify The End: famine, plague, Attila the Hun, World War II, the energy crisis. But always in history, as right now, a crisis, a collapse, even an achievement that sends us climbing to new heights, make us look back to the earth for a point of reference.

One of the most basic points of reference is the reason we've written this book: our desire to surround ourselves with the Country Look when we decorate our homes. What is the look of the country? What country do we mean? Any and all, just as America's fabric is woven of many different threads. But every countryside seems to have elements in common: the woods, wickers, and homespun fabrics we mentioned earlier. Country is also those handsome heirlooms handmade from Jean-Claude's cherry tree and cherished down through the generations. The Country Look is an attitude as well as things: it's warm, comfortable, insouciant furnishings that add up to interiors where the attitude is easy, mellow, unstudied, unmannered, unpretentious.

Between now and the back cover of this book, we intend to turn all those adjectives into practical additions to your decorating vocabulary. We'll analyze the Country Look in its many parts: colors, walls, floors, furniture, fabrics . . . every ingredient that contributes to the overall effect. And we'll tell you what to choose, where to find it, how to use it to transplant that look from yesteryear to your rooms today.

Country roads really are taking us home. The weekend retreat hidden away in the country is worth the price of getting there for many big-city dwellers who spend five days a week face to face with concrete and traffic. Lawrence Peabody, whose design business routinely takes him from Haiti to Denmark to New York and farther, says he and his wife slip off as often as possible down the back roads to their old home in Rindge, New Hampshire, opposite, above. The lure? "The warmth and richness of old woods with the patina of years of love . . . a mellowness and ambiance that is particularly American . . . real greenery everywhere, herbs drying upside-down from the rafters, candlelight, firelight, smells . . . bread being baked . . . picking the salad from the garden, making the dressing with your own herbs, and serving with love." Below, opposite, country is expressed in small ways. Weathered-wicker laundry baskets filled with geraniums march up the stone from the steps of the Peabodys' New Hampshire farmhouse.

Country is also whimsy, furnishings that don't take themselves too seriously or expect you to. This vast bath in a country house is a happy case in point. The hard, cold lines of modern conveniences have been hidden away inside the natural warmth of natural materials: woods, plaster, old-fashioned iron cast in the comforting role of a wood-burning stove. Not just for show, the stove is an energy-efficient way to keep the bathroom cozy. The whimsy coefficient comes from the bathtub masquerading as a four-poster bed canopied in calico sheets, and the sink sunk into what looks like an old dresser. Actually, it's an adaptation of an antique, manufactured by a company well aware of today's Country currents.

Country is more an attitude than the actual room in which you are expressing it. Opposite, the kitchen of a reclaimed farmhouse is allowed to flaunt its rustic past while functioning with twentieth-century efficiency. Soft-colored appliances don't distract the eye from the overall effect created by the barnwood cabinet fronts and knotty-pine beamed ceiling, used as it would have been a century ago, to store seldom-needed utensils

17

The
Country Look
Is . . .

. . . "Down-home decorating" . . . "laidback living" . . . "Country chic." No matter what you call it, *mood*, much more than actual furniture, is the common denominator of the Country Look.

We've already dusted off the *why's* behind today's emotional needs for country-style living and decorating. Now, let's explore the *what's* of the Country Look, what distinguishes it as a distinct style.

Country is eclectic, a harmonious mixture of furnishings that share the same easygoing attitude. At the same time, Country is many textures, many materials, many colors. In fact, Country is many countries, many different idioms all saying, "Come in. Feel welcome. Be comfortable."

Wood says that . . . in warm accents made mellow by years of wear and love. Or by the modern furniture manufacturer's artifice. "Distressing" is a method of finishing furniture with chains and gouges and spattered stains so that the piece is both brand-new and instantly old at the moment it emerges from the factory. Not every wood can be forced to assume a country accent, however. The exotics—zebra wood, yew, teak, rosewood, and such—almost never fit the role. Even mahogany has a hard time. Although it was widely used in American furniture as early as the 1700s, mahogany is such a hard wood it inspires delicate, sophisticated styles, elaborately carved and finished to formal splendor. This, of course, brings us smack up against the question of Victorian pieces, vigorously carved, mar-

COUNTRY IS

. . . *wicker, snatched in off the front porch and pillowed in happy patchwork.*

. . . *nostalgia, a gentler era recaptured in the lace, photographs, and flowers crowding this "front parlor" skirted table.*

. . . *simplicity, the glow of pewter and worn pine in the soft light from a beeswax candle.*

ble-topped, upholstered in deep velvets. Parlor-elegant to the eye of that era, such excesses look quaint and whimsical to us today. Thus redefined as "nostalgia," a term that also embraces Tiffany lamps, stained glass, and button-tufting, the most outrageous Victorian pieces can work in a Country atmosphere. But don't copy the true Victorians, who abhorred a void. A few such "conversation" pieces are witty additions; more simply create visual noise.

COUNTRY IS A COLLECTION . . .

. . . of antique and ersatz *family portraits and other whimsical subjects against a barn-board wall.*

. . . of antique tin canisters on a fanciful brass rack; yesteryear's trivia now turned treasures.

. . . of pillows, all lace and gingham and hand-done embroidery, adding vitality to a sunny windowseat.

And "loud" is disallowed in Country living. Flash and glint and shine are wrong; think in *glowing* terms instead. Even the woods should be down key, down home, literally; the kind of woods that grow "on the home place." That includes Jean-Claude's dower cherry and other domestic fruit-woods, plus the likes of oak, maple, and pine. Especially pine. Soft, knotty, and exuberantly grained, pine was made to order for the country craftsman of old. It was easy to come by, easy to carve, and it grew darker and richer as it took on years.

Of course, the woods that grow "on the place" depend on where the place is. Rush, cane, wicker, willow—bent and woven into fanciful shapes—all count as Country. So does a slice of any tree trunk turned into a table. And so do hand-adzed beams, bare plank floors, barn board, butcher block, and painted furniture, most of it, at least. Chinoiserie need not apply; stenciled designs, always. Again, it's *mood* we're discussing, the difference between a tiptoeing mahogany tea table and a flatfooted pine harvest table, between a painted Sheraton side chair and a stenciled Windsor, between a mirrored Art Deco cocktail table and an old trunk pressed into service before the sofa.

Color also says Country. The genesis of most authentic Country color is nature. Or *was* nature, back in the days when berries, barks, roots, onion skins, indigo, and such yielded up their natural colors in the boiling pot. Paints were concocted from earthern extracts, and woods were most often left in their own natural richness. So were fabrics. The methods may have changed but the look is still natural, still defined in terms of coarse Haitian cottons, Berber rugs, whitewashed walls, brick, slate, and deep-earth paints. But quick! Before you think Country lacks true color, think of San Blas embroidery . . . of patchwork quilts . . . Mexican pottery . . . rag rugs . . . Portuguese tiles . . . baskets full of hollyhocks and hydrangeas.

Country is indeed colorful, in both senses of the word. As country people are, of necessity, independent, so can be Country-style decorating. Anything goes into your interior if *you* like it and if it falls, however loosely, into these categories:

- It's a natural (sisal rug, cotton slipcovers, stucco walls);
- It's homemade and looks it;
- It's as utilitarian as it is pleasing to look at (a basket, a weather vane, a collection of farm tools);
- It has a sense of humor or whimsy (old medicine tins, a Victorian umbrella tree, ancestor photographs).

Although few rules still survive about decorating, period, there are absolutely none when it comes to self-expression, Country-style . . . except the *raison d'être* rule against rigidity and formality.

Country is seeing with a newly appreciative eye all the trappings from another era. Happily, the "make do or do without" attitude of Depression days lasted well into the 1950s, so attics full of put-back treasures are still up there waiting. You can also mine the flea-market circuit, wade through garage sales, and stalk the country auction for a touch of the whimsy that's so much a part of the easy Country ambiance.

23

The Color of Country

There's really only one thing to keep in mind when you set a color scheme for your Country-Look room: Nature.

The conventional approach to decorating schemes (i.e., those that revolve around complementary colors, related colors, or monochromes) is too contemporary, too studied, too "decorator correct" for the Country Look. Speaking from both historical and emotional perspective, any room where the planning shows is slicker than it should be. Such self-consciousness is simply not Country.

Eschewing conventional decorating wisdom takes you back to Nature, the nicest colorist of all. Country color schemes fall into two categories or, to make it even easier, into two seasons: Winter fields and Summer gardens.

Run your mind's eye over that for a minute and you'll know just what colors to go after.

Winter fields: Think of the mixed tans of dried grasses; the rusts and browns and darks of bare earth; of nut colors; the grays and slates of tree bark; the reds of dry oak leaves; the dark evergreens and the silvery greens of lichen and mosses.

Winter fields: Snow-white and maple-sugar color, this country dining room is Big City sophisticated. The fanback chairs around the burl Parsons table are finds from frequent weekends out in the real countryside. So is the tree branch, nature's sculpture, dramatic against the vertical shade cloth blinds.

25

These are colors for sophisticated Country rooms with contemporary overtones (the Scandinavian influence). Winter fields colors can create marvelous monochromatic schemes, i.e., one basic color played up and down the scale. *How* you play becomes very important: Be sure to weave in all the rich textures Nature puts at your fingertips, such as rugged tree bark and worn-smooth woods, rough homespun fabrics and polished slate floors, trowel-marked walls and burnished-brass lamp bases. Just take care that the textures fit the basic Country criteria: no satins, no brocades, no crystal or cut velvets. Lace should look handloomed, even gutsy; deep shag rugs are out of the question. So are chrome, plate-glass mirror, Mylar, and flocked-velvet wallcoverings. Surprising, perhaps, but sometimes acrylic and glass topped tables can be made to look at home in Country rooms because their transparency lets other textures shine through. Even the spare, square lines

Summer Gardens: An ingathering of gingham runs in happy patches all over this attic room for a little girl. Two separate wallcoverings, both of which have matching fabrics, are skillfully interwoven for a look that's far more interesting than a single pattern could be. The one element that brings it all off is color—— the same exact shade of happy pink runs through both patterns, tying them skillfully together.

Winter Fields: This is a Country kitchen as the Scandinavians might see it: richly grained wood cooled slightly in the finishing combine with touches of deep color on the far wall and in the accessories. Butcher block, baskets, and mock-mosaic tiles in monoearth tones keep the kitchen calm; the interesting horizontals of the cabinet fronts keep it from boring.

27

COUNTRY COLOR CUES

Winter Fields

The harvest is gone . . . the riotous colors of summer subdued. . . . Nature's palette is subtle, softened, hushed and restful . . . introverted, introspective. Interiors take on the same visual and emotional qualities when they take on the un-colors of *Winter Fields*. If you follow this color line, you're almost assured decorating success. There's nothing to clash, nothing to worry about matching. About the only hazard with natural-on-natural colors is boredom. To avoid it, take a second look at Nature in her winter dress and you'll find a harvest of accent colors to liven up your scheme: deep reds, as in lacquer-slick oak leaves still rustling on the branches . . . that clear bright blue that winter skies can be made of . . . the sharp surprise of fire thorn, bittersweet, and holly berries . . . the rich greens of firs, spruce, pines. . . . It's the accent color that spices a *Winter Fields* color scheme to life, but like any spice, sharp color should be used sparingly, or the accent will quickly become the dominant voice in your room.

The palette of Winter Fields colors includes:
. . . the grays and tans of weathered woods

. . . the rusts and darks
of farm tools

. . . the silvered beige
of pussy willows

Summer Gardens

Bachelor's buttons . . . goldenrod . . . hydrangeas . . . poppies in full, riotous bloom with butterflies hovering overhead . . . You're conjuring the colors of a Summer Garden in the country. In the Country Look room, the brights come out of the garden and onto the furniture, fabrics, and accessories. Although time has tended to fade and soften their colors, quilts and braided rag rugs were once as bright and sharp as their creators could manage. Homespun and handloomed fabrics were exuberant; calicoes, ginghams, and bandanna prints brought pattern and color power to yesteryear's interiors. Today's, too. And, as in Winter Fields decorating, it's not easy to make a mistake, since Country is congenial to all colors and almost all at the same time. The colors in a bouquet of wildflowers don't clash. Nor did the colors in a Country room from earlier, more naïve times. But our better-trained eye does call for some co-ordination, some color cross-referencing to offer visual order and generous spreads of the naturals to act as visual calmatives.

The color bouquet of Summer Gardens includes:
. . . the punchiness of patchwork

. . . the translucent glow
of stained glass

. . . the gay abandon
in a braided rag rug

of a Parsons table, as bone-honest as any Shaker design, will work in a Country room, but only if it's not some slick and showy color.

Texture is touch-me important when a room is based on Winter fields colors. It's this easy to be sure you include enough textural contrast: Gather a basket of pine cones for the coffee table; hang a sinewy bare tree branch over the mantel; toss a natural wool afghan on the leather love seat; lay a vinyl-brick floor, or trowel dimensional interest into a plastered wall.

Summer gardens: Gather a bouquet of wildflowers and rejoice in the profusion of colors you can choose among. But why choose at all? In its innocence, its spontaneity, Country makes room for them all. And like a patchwork quilt or braided rag rug, there's no such thing as too many colors, too much pattern, or a poor combination of them.

What *is* wrong for a Country room are broad sleek expanses of the primary colors: bright blue, red, or yellow. Downplay the dramatic, the too stimulating. Opt instead for the off-color, the soft color. Or, if you do bring in the brights from that Summer garden bouquet, bring them *all* in, or at least enough to present a pleasant potpourri. Play it à la the Impressionists, with a sunny, warm, commingling of colors that teases the eye and buoys the soul.

What texture is to color schemes based on a *Winter fields* palette, pattern is to *Summer garden* rooms. A veritable patchwork of patterns can coexist merrily as long as they share at least one obvious color. Calicoes, ginghams, batiks, bandannas—there's as much room for them all in the Country Look as there's room for all flowers in a Summer garden.

Summer Gardens bloom all over this happy quilt, opposite, above. *The flower-bed-bright colors in the linens' primitive print echo the rug and accessories. Otherwise, the background is kept plain and subtle: white walls, simple painted shutters, warm woods left natural. It's a decorating formula that's sure to succeed in coloring Country rooms.*

The best of both color worlds comes to pass in the greenhouse atmosphere of this garden room, opposite, below. *A new addition to an old farmhouse, the room stays in bloom, both literally and figuratively, all year round. The flower-scattered fabric on the rattan furniture creates the "Summer Gardens" mood even when real Winter Fields lie outside the arched glass enclosure.*

COUNTRY COLOR IS . . .

. . . down-to-Earth colors in a big city apartment.
A color collage borrowed from Winter Fields' palette
can be Uptown sophisticated in the right context.
Here, it's an old, high-ceilinged apartment
with parquet floors well worth the redeeming
that has made them too handsome now to hide.
Against the subtle Earth colors of
warm putty, loam browns, the natural woodiness
of wicker, and the tree- trunk table,
suddenly the green of
the plants—both painted and potted—becomes
the lively accent color that quickens
the visual pulse of the room.

32

COUNTRY COLOR IS...

. . . the natural warmth within the Winter Fields spectrum, the warm browns of woods, of terra cotta, and tortoise shell. Four cases in point, clockwise on the opposite page, a redwood-enriched open gallery in Fort Worth, with waxed natural cement floors and a harvest of greens; by designer Pat McMillan, this dining area is steeped in the woodsy tones of reproduction Early American furniture, all nicely spiced by the antique silk patchwork quilt-cum-art on the wall; Jan Rankin designs a kitchen corner that's cozy as morning coffee in its cocoon of provincial prints. Above, the coziness comes from the convivial clutter that designer John Hayden has orchestrated in this tiny apartment. The colors: Earth reds and browns with a surprising pinch of purple in the throw pillow. Purple!

COUNTRY COLOR IS . . .

. . . the fern greens of a forest glade in the summer,
transplanted prettily to this bed-sitting room.
Wallcovering with matching fabric does the
decorating trick in what is essentially a
monochromatic green color scheme.
White is the brightener (one-color-plus-white
schemes almost always work), with
just a flicker of red added to
keep the eye hopping happily.

A massive four-poster bed of cedar, with a plain-Jane finish, and an early Queen Anne chair point up the easygoing eclecticism that is a keynote of furnishing country style. A scarcity of pieces, which creates a kind of Spartan simplicity, is also associated with the Country look, especially evocative of Shaker interiors. There, as in this photograph, utility was important, and each piece had to "earn its keep."

Country Furniture

Country furniture is sturdy woods, punched-tin doors, space-saving tables, and chairs that rock. It's sometimes awkward, but always sincere—with no veneer to help disguise designed-for-duty pieces. It's the common garden variety of that swell-elegant furniture that may follow the form but lacks the fancy carving, veneers, and elaborate ornamentation of big-city furniture. More than just Early American or French Provincial, country furniture the world over was made by regional craftsmen for rural people. Today, the peasant-style furniture, with the guileless charm of poor proportions and whimsical decoration, helps create pastoral ambiance, in town and out.

Furniture for the Country mood comes from many sources: Hand-me-down; found (in attic, basement or barn); sought—at Salvation Army stores, estate sales or auction; store-bought—from your favorite furniture store or antique shop.

Important to the Country feeling is a wonderfully worn look. The most authentic rooms result when furniture is simply gathered and gleaned from hither and yon. However, many newly manufactured reproductions recapture the charm of the old.

Untangling the lineages of Country styles may not be essential, since most provincial styles mix and mingle easily with their Country counterparts. But understanding origins can be helpful, and roots of enduringly popular provincial styles are easy to trace.

FRENCH PROVINCIAL. One of the most enduringly popular is the provincial French furniture made by craftsmen through various regions of France, of such woods as oak, chestnut, beech, elm, cherry, pear, and plum. Pieces were copied from court furniture produced during the reigns of the Louis from XIII to XVI. The style of Louis XV, with its graceful "S" curves, has proven most popular throughout France and the world. Country styles are often left unfinished, with waxed surfaces making the most of natural graining.

"Clothes make the man"—and sometimes the furniture too! Give upholstered pieces a country look by covering them in a "country" fabric. Here two wing chairs and a camelback sofa with city ways take on Country airs when they are upholstered in pretty patchwork and co-ordinating calico. Quilting provides extra strength for fabrics like calico and gingham. The iron stove, an important piece of functioning furniture in earlier days, merely adds to the ambiance in this room by designers Abby Darer and Bobbi Stuart. However, the energy crunch has revived interest in alternate methods of home heating, and brand-new old styles are back on the market.

EARLY AMERICAN. Furniture made in America's early colonial days (1608–1725) has a rustic, rugged simplicity that especially connotes "Country." This American Colonial (or Early American) furniture was based largely on remembered English medieval forms of the Tudor, Elizabethan, and Jacobean eras.

PENNSYLVANIA DUTCH (1680–1850). Made by Swiss and German immigrants who settled eastern Pennsylvania, New Jersey, and southern New York, so-called "Pennsylvania Dutch" (from "Deutsch," meaning German) has a lot in common with English-inspired Early American furniture and mixes well with it.

AMERICAN FRONTIER (1690–1890). This crude, homemade, and now-charming furniture was created by early Midwest settlers, mountaineers, frontiersmen, and ranchers. Unable to fit furniture into the wagons they crossed the mountains in, the settlers made their own once they got to the other end of the line. Included were novel wagon-seat benches and horn chairs, highback settles, drysinks, cupboards, and cobblers' benches.

SHAKER (1775–1850). Shaker furniture, with its Spartan plainness and elegant severity, lends a dignified feeling to today's interiors.

MEDITERRANEAN. Another style which contributes to the casual Country mood is the vigorous and masculine, darkly finished Mediterranean style.

MISSION OAK furniture, originating in California and popular from 1895–1910, was simple, square, extremely sturdy, and utterly without decoration.

GOLDEN OAK. Machine-made and mass-marketed oak furniture of the late 1860s and early 1900s wore the quaint carvings and turnings copied from "fine" furniture by designers traveling from city to city.

PRIMITIVE FORMS—TWIG AND TREE TRUNK. Twig furniture, made from willow branches wrapped and tied into fanciful forms, was once reserved for the southern lawn and cabin porch. Recently rediscovered in the mid-seventies by designers delighted with its unorthodox shapes, twig furniture seems right at home in humble-pie or Country-chic surroundings. Today's counterpart—only much more heroic in scale—is the tree trunk, cut down to serve as Bunyanesque chairs, tables, and four-posters.

WICKER, BAMBOO, AND RATTAN, formerly porch furniture, has also come in out of the weather. Their woven texture and graceful forms mix easily and excitingly with other woods, wrought iron, even brass or chrome.

PERSONALITY PIECES

Form in country furniture really did follow function. Accentuate a positive Country flavor in any room by adding a piece of furniture that's as useful as it is decorative. In these rooms, a slant-top desk-and-hutch with tote-along stool, a tray-top coffee table, an apothecary chest, multipurpose hall piece (complete with seat, hooks, and mirror), or a simple, Shaker-influenced silver chest provide added Country oomph . . . and are just as practical today as when our space-shy forebears first crafted them.

39

Furniture can compensate for the absence of architectural details in today's structures. In this bedroom, architectural interest is provided by the tester bed with paneled headboard and the deeply carved armoire. The strong influence of bed and armoire is underscored by the plank-top table/desk and the ladderback chair, all derived from early Canadian furniture styles. A wing chair, stenciled floor, and patterned fabric, covering table, bed, and walls, play up the provincial theme.

Pure and simple lines, surfaces devoid of decoration, and a clear pine finish give this furniture a "fresh from the tree" look that would be at home in any country cottage. The ready-to-assemble sleeping platform is surrounded by stackable storage units that can be arranged in any number of configurations to suit the rugged individualist. A bright plaid fabric and boldly colored rug and walls contrast handsomely with the quiet of the natural-wood finish.

41

Country clues in these three rooms: windows with a nude look and bare floors with a swept-clean glint. Over all, furniture has little in common—which is a common characteristic of much of the furniture we call "Country." Here, a horn chair with its right-off-the-range look, the oval table with double-pedestal base in light-oak finish, and a scalloped-top cabinet, sitting cater-cornered to save wall space, are delightful proof that a great variety of furniture can play the Country game.

43

TEXTURES

*Get back to nature's most basic ma-
terials—woven cane or rush—for
real textural interest in a Country
room. They can join forces with
other natural materials, e.g., tree
bark, Haitian cotton, or New England pine, with equal aplomb.*

46   *Chairs descended from French provincial ancestors star in this kitchen-cum-greenhouse. Wearing an antiqued finish and rush bottom, these tall ladderbacks pit cheerful, curved lines against more sober straight lines of the do-it-yourself table.*

Simple lines and unadorned surfaces give this Shaker-inspired dining group, above, an easy-to-live-with dignity. Crisp red-and-white gingham adds snap, crackle, and provincial pop, while the navy-blue enameled lighting fixtures contribute to the patriotic color scheme.

Originally, country furniture was homemade, not "store-bought." The kitchen, above, carries on the made-at-home tradition with a dining nook shaped from knotty pine. Fine finishing work is not expected in Country interiors, where a kind of unself-conscious crudeness contributes to the down-home mood.

Quaint rush-bottomed corner chairs in a light pine finish pull up to a no-non-sense work-and-serve table in the well-planned kitchen, above. Open shelves and painted beams restate the Country message, echoed by the lighting fixture and pieces of pottery.

Country summers are practically synonymous with baskets of flowers straight from the garden. Romantic wicker, with its handcrafted, textured woven-basket look, and fabrics with backyard botanical designs capture the summer-garden fantasy in this charming but thoroughly practical nursery. The furniture, all from Grandma's attic, gains a go-together feeling with a coat of lead-free white paint. The old wooden floor was slicked with white paint, then sprays of flowers inspired by the fabric were drawn on with freehand abandon. A clear acrylic final coat creates the hard-as-nails finish that can cope with crayons, doll carriages, and young friends who spill their tea.

50

Wicker weaves a special kind of Country magic that recalls warm summer nights on wide front porches. Paired with playful prints, wicker is especially wonderful in garden rooms, nurseries, and bedrooms and/or on porches, whether open or enclosed. Whether painted or left natural, wicker is versatile: It is comfortable with pretty prints, with handsome solids like Haitian cotton, or with any number of other fabrics.

Country is not a matter of geography, it's a state of mind. The Shakers would have applauded the simplicity of the dining room, above, where the rectilinear lines of the glass-top table echo those of ladderback chairs which wear a company's-coming coat of antique-blue paint. The dramatic patchwork-patterned hanging is actually an area rug. Inside double Dutch doors, top right, a country kind of out-of-doors indoors ambiance is amplified by the plank-top table, surrounded by `low, curved-back, rush-bottomed chairs. The designer of a Boston townhouse, bottom right, parlays parquet floors and a French country kitchen table into a winning provincial setting. The provincial attitude is underscored by a pair of Regency dining chairs and a banquette, covered in purely practical, leather-look Naugahyde.

52

COUNTRY FURNITURE
IS ECLECTIC

Armor is out and linens are in, in an old armoire, top left, which is lined with a ribbon-and-sprig wallcovering. Like its original provincial ancestors, it wears a coat of paint to hide common (hence "inferior") wood. Wicker baskets serving as cachepots are a provincial ploy. A Victorian version Country-style bedroom, bottom left, boasts a massive brass bed topped with a sheepskin throw to ward off winter chills. Underfoot, a varicolored shaggy rug in a random pattern marks the informal mood. Cane-back chairs, a round dining table, and a marble-topped chest with ceramic knobs, say Country in the room above. The message is re-stated in curtainless windows, the bare brick wall, and lots of white woodwork.

55

Country takes us "back to basics," and what could be more basic than twig furniture? Once welcome only on lawn or porch, this primitive furniture has captured the fancy of Country-lovers everywhere for use anywhere about the house. Rustic, whimsical, a wonderful foil for posh, print-covered pillows, twig and bent-willow furniture has come a long way since its Depression-days heydays in the hands of semiskilled farmers. Furniture like that in the loft bedroom, opposite, brings back nostalgic recollections of yesteryear's front-parlor days and gussied-up ways. Adaptable, it can be dressed up or down, depending on your choice of accessories and appointments.

Floors—
Country Underfoot

Your floors play the major supporting role for everything that adds up to the Country ambiance you are after in your rooms. Happily, you can create the right feeling in your flooring without being authentic. We say "happily," since the first floors were, doubtless, made of plain old hard-packed dirt. Early alternatives to that were wide-board floors, brick, or stone. Hard-surface flooring materials today still include the real things—wood, brick, stone, mosaic and ceramic tile, all in keeping with country living. Then there are also resilient floorings of vinyl and vinyl asbestos that look, for all the world, like real wood and brick and stone but are far easier to pay for, to install anywhere, and to live with underfoot. In addition to being lookalikes for natural materials, resilient floorings offer a plethora of other Country-compatible looks. A Dutch-tile pattern in Delft colors can play up the theme of a room filled with Pennsylvania Dutch-style furniture. Synthetic tile with a quarried look says "Country" with an-almost-real southwestern drawl. It won't be quite as authentic as the real McCoy, nor will it last as long, but it will be easier on the feet. You can lay it anywhere—in a basement, in an apartment, for example—and do the work yourself. For a room with a hoedown feeling, put down tiles or sheet goods in a happy bandanna print. It will do more than hint at a down-on-a-midwestern-farm feeling.

Appropriate soft floorings for Country rooms include wall-to-wall carpeting, and room-size and small area rugs. Often, hard and soft floorings are used together. For example, a room-size or area rug may be used over wood, brick, stone, or tile floorings. Occasionally, soft-surface floorings are used together; that is, a decorative area rug will be placed over wall-to-wall carpeting to create areas of special interest.

For other rooms with the flavor of specific country regions, follow the floorings favored in those regions. For example, in a sitting room with a New England flavor, choose wide-board floors accented with braided rag or Oriental area rugs. Or, if authenticity is not important, be fancy free. Instead of an Oriental rug, use one with a Navaho design. Or, instead of wooden floors, use wall-to-wall carpeting with a braided rug design, or with the pattern of antique brick. Better still, throw caution to the proverbial winds and choose a resilient flooring in a patchwork-quilt pattern. Remember, our ancestors simply didn't have all our options.

Still, exercising some of those options can undermine your Country mood. Too slick and too citified are such no-no's as deep shags, bold abstract prints, elaborate parquet, too-fancy marble, and terrazza floors.

Nothing says "Country" quite so quickly as an expanse of bare hardwood floor graced with a prized Oriental rug.

BRICK
THREE
WAYS

Brick floors are as Country as a garden path. And today, whether you want them 61
real or faux, you can have it your way. Antique pavers add warmth of color and
texture to the breakfast nook, top left, while a nylon carpet with brick pattern
and coloration underscores the cozy Country feeling of the family room, bottom
left. Modern technology marries a brick pattern to cushioned vinyl in the
kitchen, above, for the best of both worlds—yesterday's charm and today's easy
maintenance.

"Country" in the great southwestern style means generously scaled ceramic tile floors, which give the warmth and color of desert sands and ask only to be damp-mopped, when needed. The contrasting grout repeats the color of stuccoed walls. New Englanders relied on wide boards for flooring and their waxed surfaces gleamed in the light of many a wintry evening's fire. The look—but not the work —of those early wood floors is available today in easy-to-keep vinyl like that in the dining room, opposite.

COUNTRY COLOR IS . . .

. . . Summer Gardens yielding up armloads of cornflowers, the color inspiration for this young-again attic room. In every pattern possible, the right bright blue scampers all over the many-angled walls and onto the frumpy fun chair and well-ruffled bed. This is an attic room refurbished with love on Mother's sewing machine, a blue room to feel anything but in.

64

COUNTRY
COLOR IS…

…a Summer Garden of colors and patterns, flourishing, right, in the Connecticut home of actress Meg Mundy. Down home up and under the eaves, the bedroom takes a helping of crewel-print wallcovering with the bolder dash of red around the swag and store-bought roller shade. Unstudied, it's the kind of ingenuous atmosphere that brings back childhood summers spent with aunts in the country.

COUNTRY IS . . . *cozy colors and cozy corners, no matter what country you're decorating à la mode of. Right, you can't get much more Country U.S.A. than bent-willow and tree-stump furniture, old backwoods crafts that have now come forth as fashion finds for the Country Look. With a Country French accent,* below, *the furniture is carved and cane-backed in imitation of court-style elegance. But the copies are ingenuous, here ingeniously finished with a light wash and do-it-yourself freehand drawings done with felt-tipped pens.*

COUNTRY IS ALSO . . . *open to many interpretations within many spatial limitations. And that includes the seemingly limitless space sprawling outside designer Jack Denst's country home in Indiana,* below. *All that natural exterior beauty gets the nod; inside, even the furniture's distilled to a low marble table and exuberantly tassled floor pillows, plus a double helping of a Denst-designed wall mural.* Above, *the ambiance's equally* au naturel *but the mood's inward-looking when you get to the carriage house that designer Allen Scruggs calls home in New Jersey. The actual outside view is much less interesting than the natural beauty inside: old leather, punched tin, tactile tweeds, hemp, and muslin, and the flat-weave native rug.*

COUNTRY IS MORE STILL . . .
here's another porch, another approach from
a perspective quite different than Jack Denst's
on the page you just turned. Designer/author
Pat McMillan recognizes the potential
in her linen closet and lets it all hang out,
literally, on the open porch of her own home
in Cornwall-on-Hudson, New York. It takes two
quick seams to shirr the sheets on rods,
and they simply wedge between the posts;
tiebacks are store-bought;
the wicker chairs wear the ordinary
bed pillows in ordinary pillow cases.
Fast, easy, and fresh as a breeze,
her ideas are yours for the stealing.

THE FOCUS
IS THE FLOOR

Don't be floored by unattractive, no-theme floors. Pick a pattern that looks country, like this cushioned vinyl with an authentic antique quilt design, and let it mosey from the kitchen right on into the dining area. One pattern used in both spaces will make this small city-apartment area look bigger than a country mile.

Broadloom carpet with a braided-rug look is a great boon to Country-style living in small spaces. Laid wall-to-wall, the carpeting is room- and even house-expanding, since it allows for continuity and, at the same time, permits a change of color schemes from room to room. Simply pick a different one of its any colors to decorate around in each room. Braided rugs, once the farm wife's way of recycling fabrics from worn-out clothing, are continuing favorite room-brighteners. They come in round and oval shapes like the one in the family room, opposite, and look great atop wood, tile, brick, or vinyl flooring.

68

Wall-to-wall carpeting with a sheepskin color and texture forms a handsome
backdrop for a carved-door armoire and oak Windsor chairs, top left, where
patchwork upholstery and accessories add Country accents. Country can be chic,
as the sisal flooring, bottom left, proves, in a living room made almost city-slick
by classic furniture. Above, a spatter-painted pattern is an easy do-it-yourself solution to time-worn floors in this attic-cum-TV-guest room. A round, sisal area rug
and antique trunk turned coffee table create the focal point around which the
country furnishings revolve.

71

Here's a sure Country remedy for ailing floors—disguise rough, rugged floorboards with painted planks given a random stencil motif inspired by the wallcovering. To preserve the message, coat with several layers of acrylic, letting each dry thoroughly between. Don't worry if your stenciling is a little crude, often naïvete was —and is—the essence of Country charm. Nothing's nicer than plain floors, opposite.

Among the many choices of rustic flooring are tiles with a quarried look. The hard, firm look of the tile floor is softened, above, with an area rug whose provincial motif is repeated in a stenciled "frame" around the entry.

New and readily available stencil kits make it easy even for a teenager to paint wall-to-wall posies on a floor. Here, they are up-scaled versions of those on curtains and spread. All that's required is the kit, a little time, and patience.

Traditional materials give a new kitchen instant "age." Built-ins, above, borrow their style from old freestanding cabinets, while the synthetic flooring imitates an ages-old herringbone brick. Two pluses from the twentieth-century: the ease to which today's synthetic floors treat your feet and the ease with which they can be maintained.

Even real, old Country-look kitchens need a little brightening. This one gains a new lease on life from the powerful provincial pattern on the new vinyl flooring. The small, all over print fabric, which skirts the work counter, adds to the pattern play, which adds up to an updated existence for what had been a servant's kitchen in the I. W. Woolworth estate on Long Island, New York.

The view from the top shows that no matter how casual the mood, there's a flooring to match. Above, a highrise bedroom can take on a Country air and a masculine mood simultaneously—just carpet it in a bold plaid. Top, opposite, for a Country bath with lots of floor space to cover, add a twentieth-century vinyl flooring that comes in an eighteenth-century pegged-board pattern. Right, faux fieldstone implies that the stable is only a stone's throw from the door.

When this country was new, Oriental area rugs were highly prized. Too precious to be allowed on the floor, they were draped across tables like works of art to be admired. Gradually, as the colonies flourished, rugs were returned to the floor. Here, an area rug with a peasant motif brightens a breakfast nook where "Country" and "clutter" are synonymous. Pebbles from a brook inspire the pattern of the easy-to-keep synthetic flooring with a lighthearted look in the kitchen, opposite. The larger-scaled random pattern of the flooring forms an interesting backdrop for the calico tablecloth and wallcovering.

In a New York City brownstone, opposite, a bare narrow-board floor, stained a rich dark brown and adorned by a bearskin rug, carries on the tradition of earlier country-home floors. In a similar vein, a parquet floor in a townhouse-cum-country manor, above, is topped with an Oriental prayer rug. Tongue-in-cheek touches to the interior include an old porch column and the twig table with glass top.

Ceilings— Country Overhead

Too often in decorating, ceilings are simply painted white or light to make them look higher, then they are forgotten, to languish overhead, contributing little to the overall effect and claiming no attention for themselves. But the sky's the limit when it comes to decorating ceilings Country-style. The imagination can take wings, basing its flight of fancy on past examples or breaking new ground to create entirely new effects.

Looking back at some past examples, we find early country cottages with ceilings merely the exposed underside of the roof. Baskets and drying herbs and plants were hung handily from beams and rafters, adding to the "busyness" and interest of ceiling and room. Later on, ceilings were covered over with materials which hid the structural elements, then were painted, and that was that. Next, ceilings were treated to plaster designs, or they were covered with decorative papers, or they were enlivened with stenciled paintings. Beams were rediscovered, this time for purely decorative reasons, and were sometimes stained dark, often painted a fetching color, and other times stenciled for added effect. The areas between beams were painted or papered. Today, *faux* beams, made of lightweight molded polyurethane and simply glued to the ceiling, look like the real thing but are so much easier to install. Special "beam" effects can be achieved by the do-it-yourselfer. One technique is to build a trough of three 1-by-4 inch boards and then nail the trough to a 1-by-4-inch board, which has been attached platelike to the ceiling. Another beam look is achieved by nailing 1-by-4-inch board flat to the ceiling with quarter-round molding along either side.

Especially attractive ceiling effects can be accomplished with wallcoverings: Cover a ceiling in a non-directional pattern that's co-ordinated with

Ceilings, often a visual wasteland, are entitled to attention-getting treatments like that in the kitchen, above. A great expanse of ceiling in large rooms like this one demands some detail. Here, an applied acoustical ceiling with a pegged-plank pattern offers pattern and textural interest, plus some degree of noise control.

the pattern on walls. A narrow ceiling molding serves as a line of demarcation. Or, try papering only the ceiling for a cozy, enclosing effect.

To give ceilings an airy summer garden or gazebo effect, paint and then cover them with treillage in a crisp Country white or garden green. Acoustical ceiling tiles, in many different patterns and colors, are available to today's Country-loving home decorators. Several patterns are especially designed to enhance the casual Country mood, emulating random wood planks, pressed tin and stucco overhead.

Real wood ceilings can be planned in many different, engaging designs, and stucco-textured paint often solves both visual and decorative problems in one fell swipe of the trowel: its rough texture hides inherent blemishes while adding authenticity overhead.

Pressed tin, a nineteenth-century ceiling staple, is another ceiling material in demand among nostalgia buffs. Also high on the overhead-interest charts are ceiling fans that enhance the very atmosphere they help to cool.

If it's the other way around—i.e., warm—that you want things, warm up a room by lowering the ceiling. Rather, lower the look of the ceiling by painting it a warm dark color. Not black, but a rich brown, deep blue, or even green overhead tends to bring a too-soaring ceiling down to heights that are cozier and more in keeping with Country taste levels.

There's something basically warm and reassuring about wooden ceilings, whether they are as simple as the exposed beam ceiling, opposite, or as intricate and decorative as that in the family room, above. Wooden ceilings give these two homes a vacation-home atmosphere—sophisticated and knowing, but very nice to live under.

87

Wallpapers that wander off the walls and onto overhead areas can contribute important decorative interest to Country rooms. Paper to match that on the dado is used between homemade ceiling beams, top left, to give the kitchen an intimate Country feeling. Lower left, a plate shelf calls attention to the unusual cornice and ceiling treatment in the dining room. The cornice, papered to match the ceiling, is emphasized by molding painted the dark brown of the chair rail below. In the attic bedroom, above, three variations on the same theme cover the walls. The interesting angles attract, but don't distract, the eye.

89

The unusual slants and slopes of this bedroom ceiling in California country are punctuated with strips of board which add a decorative touch. Wooden ceiling and walls provide pleasant contrast to the magnificent patchwork quilt and shawl wall hanging, which pit playful pattern against plain surfaces.

Early country houses were small and needed just one "summer" beam—the major roof support system that ran the room's length and rested its immense weight on the fireplace. Today's houses are larger, and lower-level game rooms can feature two or more beams, more for decorative than practical reasons. Make the most of such handsome beams: Stain them dark or paint them a bold color. To "raise" the ceiling between beams, paint the space a light color. Conversely, papering or painting the space a darker value will tend to lower the ceiling and create a more intimate feeling.

91

Exposed ceiling members produce different patterns and effects in these four rooms. In the kitchen at the top of the page, lengthwise and crosswise "beams" create a coffered look. Exposed trusswork in the kitchen, above, gives the room a big-barn look. The eye is carried rhythmically across the ceiling in the family room, top right. In another kitchen, space is found between faux beams and tile ceiling in which to stash the cook's baskets—storage in keeping with old country traditions.

Country and vertical blinds . . . the combination's not as incongruous as you might have imagined before you saw this photograph. The blinds are the perfect solution to a glassed-in sun porch that opens to the patio—and was open to all the elements. Stark and uncomplicated, they provide a plain background for the Countryness of the room, with its herringbone-vinyl floor, quilt table-dressing, and informalized Queen Anne chairs.

94

Windows with Country Views

Time was when the country outside dictated the way windows looked within. Heavy wood shutters, slatted blinds, strap-hung curtains, and simple cafes were all natural answers to the elements. There was no time to be mannered, less need to be decorative. Authentic Country window treatments are honest, purposeful, appropriate to the mood in the rest of the room; so today, it's the view *inside* that dictates the way Country windows should be dressed. Nevermind that what's *scene* through the window may be a big-cityscape or suburban street.

Still, uptight accuracy is the antithesis of Country decorating, where the whole idea is to be easy, comfortable, practical, i.e., offering control over light, elements, and privacy with the least possible fuss. Into this category fall:

· Wooden shutters, either solid, louvered, or shaped and filled with fabric insets.

· Simple curtains. Stay away from lined, pleated draperies, inherently too formal for most Country living, and stay away from most embellishments: tassels, fringes, swags, and jabots. There are some exceptions to this no-no list, and we'll show and tell why on the upcoming pages. But in gen-

COUNTRY CASUAL WINDOWS

COUNTRY CASUAL WINDOWS . . . *petticoat eyelet and bows perk up a pair of plain windows in a petit bedroom, above. The charming window wear is do-it-yourself easy, too, since the curtains come, pre-embroidered, by the yard, and the window shades are store-bought. A floral motif snipped from the wall-covering and glued-on takes away any everyday look. Opposite page, pattern, pattern everywhere picks this suburban bedroom up out of the ordinary. Much as country women used every fabric scrap for patchwork quilts, designer Frederick Twist has combined a scrapbook of different calicoes, plaids, and prints. A common color line ties them all together, from the extroverted plaid walls to the checkered tablecloth and tier-upon-tier curtains, used over a solid-color window shade trimmed in important braid.*

ANTIQUES

Ruffles and flourishes are instant refreshment for this trio of simply dressed windows. Above, gathered curtains tie back to show off gathered cafes in fabric to match the wild-animal wallcovering. Opposite page, top, the window in an old kitchen goes witty with a triple treatment of bow ribbons on the soft valance, scalloped to match the solid-color window shade beneath. The kitchen's Countryness, by the way, comes from the ship's-lath-paneled cabinets and blue and white tiles, both added during a recent remodeling.

Opposite, another remodeling job reverts a contemporary kitchen to old-time country with just-for-show beams and snap-in window grilles under the creamy froth of ruffled linen curtains.

eral, plain curtains, made of plebeian fabrics, are most in keeping with Country windows. The headings can be gathered, shirred, even smocked and ruffled. If it's casual and lighthearted, the look is right. Also appropriate: strap headings, especially on short cafes, and panels of plain fabric or lace hung flat against the window panes.

· Shades and blinds are both authentic and appropriate when they, too, are handled offhandedly, e.g., laminated with fabrics, stencil-painted, or edged with braid, ball fringe, or ruffles. Even such modern amenities as vertical blinds can look at home in the Country context. They're spare and efficient enough to recall the Shaker credo.

· Novelty treatments. Old-fashioned ingenuity has its place at Country windows, provided it stays within the bounds of good taste. That means, not cute, now overdrawn, not too eye-catching. The raison d'être for any window treatment, remember, is light and privacy control, not entertainment, and that's especially true for windows in rooms where you want to encourage the casualness in the Country attitude.

SUNDAY-BEST WINDOWS for Country rooms with upscale ambitions. Even out in the provinces, some country people liked to put on city airs and parlor manners. Here, the windows follow suit with the simplest cornice and jabot idea, opposite page, in a room designed by Margot Gunther. The tea table and chairs are antiques; the grand grandfather clock, rug, and clean, fresh window treatment are re-creations of earlier elegance. A breezy kind of nonchalance sets the hunting-lodge mood of the Country room, above. Only it's in the heart of Manhattan, not in the forests of Europe. Ordinarily, the allover pattern look is too twentieth-century to carry off a Country look, but here that pattern is two appropriate subjects, birds and flowers, used with a flourish on gathered valances, ruffled curtains, saucy slipcovers, and all the walls between.

MORE SUNDAY-BEST DRESSED WINDOWS. Above, *crewel is kind to the window wall in a one-room apartment that works around the clock. With every inch precious, there was no space to waste on elaborate window dress. The shades, laminated with the same crewel used on sofa and bedspread, tuck away behind double-hung shutters that also conceal an air conditioner. Handsome is as handsome does. Opposite page, a normally formal swag becomes something casually tossed off over a wooden rod and given bouncy ball fringe for a final informal touch.*

TAKE-IT-EASY WINDOW IDEAS

The wonder of Country-style windows is how easy they can be to dress. Leave the elaborate layers to the French Louis, the complex cornices and swags and such to the Victorians. Country windows are meant to be uncomplicated and easygoing. Here come some samples of the simplicity we have in mind, windows worth copying in your own Country rooms.

To wit, this window, opposite page, is pushpin easy. In this 1864 carriage-house living room, designer Allen Scruggs has swagged panels of unbleached muslin on large pushpins inserted through grommets set into the tops of the panels. The tiebacks and bottom trim on the muslin are souvenirs from the designer's travels —Afghani horse rope made of goat and camel's hair interwoven with wool. The rug, also Afghani, supplies the design motif custom-cut into the bottom of the window shade used under the no-sew draperies. Below, there's no sewing, no nothing, in fact, to this window treatment where sunshine for the plants is more important than privacy for the people. There is a Venetian blind for nocturnal duty; otherwise, the window is worn bare in the open-country manner, with only a few plants to green-up the scene.

Easiest Country Ways with Windows: Leave them nude, opposite page, below, when the scenery deserves it. Or settle for simple roller shades, those old-fashioned favorites that can take on many great new looks: opposite, top, they're tiger-lily bright with added-on trimming. Above, this page, a window shade has been brightened with laminated-on fabric to match the winsome clover wallcovering (there's a do-it-yourself kit to make it easy and inexpensive). The lushly ruffled percale overcurtains add essential softness to the window area in this tiny, tiny bedroom alcove. Right, a bright corner with no view is turned into a tiny interior garden using latticework set inside the picture windows to screen the no-scene. In the shallow space between the cafe curtains and trellis flourishes a harvest of house plants.

EASIEST COUNTRY WINDOW IDEAS

Shutters, pure and simple, are exactly right for the towering windows in this re-modeled townhouse, opposite page. The shutters open to frame the window areas and add important width to their verticality. Closed, the shutters would offer ab-solute privacy, but that's seldom necessary since the windows also wear unusual see-through roller shades. Made of Fiberglas mesh, the shades block outside eyes during the day, but let insiders see out. To break up all that expanse of white, designer Arthur Leaman has added a glass shelf at sash level to hold plants up to the just-right light that now filters in. Above, this window is an open-and-shut basket case. Noted designer Larry Peabody has made practical and tactile use of the space around the kitchen window in his New Hampshire farmhouse. And all you need is a hammer and a bushel of baskets to nail down his idea for your own home.

Too handsome to hide, this attic window is dressed from the waist down only, so the leaded-glass arch shows in all its frosted glory. Two wedge-in spring-tension rods hold the short curtain tautly in place, so the whole treatment is a snap to make; pun intended.

WINDOW PAINS

Windows, like people, come in all sizes and shapes, presenting all kinds of problems when time comes to get them dressed. But no matter what shape they're in—bay, bow, arched, attic, wall-to-wall, or very small—the right rods can take the pains out of dressing problem windows Country-style.

Here's an easy guide to the helpful hardware you'll find on your dealer's shelves or in his custom-order catalogues.

· Bow windows—you can custom-order all kinds of rods to fit the curve, e.g., single stationary rods, traverse rods, combination stationary and traverse rods to hold a valance or cornice over draperies that draw.

· Bay windows—ordinary extension rods can be used, one for each angle of the bay, or you can buy special three-sided rods that adjust to fit all the angles.

· Arched windows—look for a flexible eyelet rodding that bends to fit the window's curve.

· Attic dormers—a spring tension rod makes easy work of these tight spaces. Simply wedge it into the window.

· French doors—sash rods and swinging rods for both stationary and draw curtains solve French door problems *très* fast.

· Corner windows—panes that meet in the corner can be pains, indeed. Soothe and solve them with custom-bent, right-angle traverse rods or with stay-put, right-angle rods that extend in both directions to fit any corner.

111

The solution to this double problem window is made in the shades. A pair of them, black and braid-trimmed, dress both the ordinary window and the door to the patio outside this city brownstone living room-study. Framed top-to-floor walnut shutters fold in to obliterate the problem completely, including the through-the-wall air conditioner under the window. Folded open, the shutters frame the just-for-fun antique stove, reincarnated here as a plant stand.

The illusions of grandeur up under the eaves in this reclaimed attic bath come from the self-sticking mirror tiles that make a faux window over the tub. The real window, a narrow little thing, wears homemade board shutters, covered to match the walls and framed with nailed-on lathing strips. The built-in tub is another illusion from designer Bic Johnson's bag of tricks: The tub sits in a plywood frame, bricked, like the floor, in self-adhering vinyl tiles.

Another double helping of wallcovering and companion fabric dresses this small window, awkwardly placed over the bathroom vanity. With privacy of the utmost importance, designer Ann Heller had to pull out all the stops: First, there are short fabric-filled shutters, then comes a laminated window shade (you can do it yourself with a kit). Overall there's a small board cornice, covered in fabric to carry on the pattern-play and hide the shade's roller in the process.

AWKWARD
SHAPES

Arched or elongated, unusual window shapes call for creative solutions like the trio of treatments on these pages. Opposite page, top, a built-in beauty of a window required a carpenter to cope. When the kitchen was remodeled to give it Country character, the windows were framed in and fitted with shaped shutters to match the new cabinet fronts. Bottom, the arch is smaller but not the problem in this pretty bedroom window with leaded stained glass. Once again, it's shutters to the rescue, this time folding panels covered in the happy patchwork of the walls and emboldened with added molding. Above, a wall-to-wall apartment window is a giant-sized challenge but no match for designer Allen Scruggs. He as bridged the expanse with a cornice board covered in crewel, then treated the single wide window in three equal parts, with shaped roller shades and hourglass curtains caught to the windowsill on sash rods.

115

AT BAY

Held at bay by a window? Study all the angles in these three clever solutions to bay-window dressing. Above, designer-author Pat McMillan puts a small bay to work in a big way: She tops the built-in storage cabinets with a bed of gravel so a plant forest can flourish there. Side draperies soften the look; a wide, wide window shade insures privacy in the sitting-dining room. Opposite page, top, a bayful of berries makes dining delightful on a banquette built into the window. The view's so super, a valance is the only required dressing by day; by night, the draw draperies come into play. Bottom, bay for bathing calls for a clever combo of treatments. For complete privacy, short sheer cafes meet roller shades. The candy-striped stationary draperies and overall valance are merely window dressing, pure and pretty.

117

Ways with window seats: Who doesn't cherish the notion of napping in a sun-warmed seat beneath a pride of windows? But who knows how to dress the area for the occasion? Designer-author Pat McMillan for one. In her own dining room, opposite, top, she's encouraged the French accent inherent in the shaped, painted lambrequin that soars over the window seat. Glued-on ribbon plays homage to the French tricoleurs, echoed everywhere from the curtains bow-tied over the tiny sheer cafes to the melange of blue print pillows. Opposite, bottom, a keeping-room kitchen boasts a lounge area for kibitzers, built in under the once-wall-to-wall window. For architectural importance, wooden arches have been added and covered in the same peppy provincial print used throughout the room. Above, giving up to gain space, designer Shirley Regendahl built bookshelves on both sides of the window, then evened things out by adding the window seat between.

Window dressings with hidden dividends, both these shade treatments Countrify rooms while covering problems. Opposite page, it's an air conditioner that needs to be out of sight and mind for whole seasons at a time. Draw down the super-sized window shade and the unit disappears neatly behind the seashells cut out from scraps of wallcovering. Above, shades-plus-curtains spread beauty over a beastly ugly radiator under the window in this flower-fresh retreat for a growing girl. The solid-color vinyl-coated shades are trimmed in glued-on ruffles made from the same bright print that skirts the radiator issue and dresses the bed to boot.

Paneling, with all the look and feel of weathered barn board, and rugged field-stone join forces to create the background for this comfortable living room that's unmistakably in the Country. Wing and Windsor chairs may hint at Early America, but the architecture says something about contemporary America and our fondness for barn-sized soaring spaces caught within "natural" boundaries.

Walls that Wrap Country Around You

Country walls may be just about anything but smooth and shiny! They may be wood—knotty pine, vertical or horizontal cedar or pine planks, cedar shakes, barn board, or even board-and-batten come in from the cold. They may be exposed brick, fieldstone, rough plaster, or textured paint. They can be covered in linen, burlap, or denim. Some may wear provincially patterned ceramic tile; others, paper. The point is, Country walls are never plain. And while they should not be "fancy," Country walls must be treated to either texture or pattern or some combination of these elements.

If you take the "naturals" route to Country decorating, you'll find a wealth of woods from which to choose a background that gets your room back to basics. Traditionalists will hearken to knotty pine or cedar boards applied vertically. The less conventional can look to cedar shakes or barn board for a more rustic touch. Board-and-batten, originally used on exteriors, is now perfectly welcome indoors, where its vertical stripe effect tends to heighten too-low ceilings.

Many 4-by-8-foot wood panels make it easy for the do-it-yourselfer to give walls a Country look. They come in a wide variety of wood grains and colors and in a wide range of textures. As a guide, use the rougher textures with heavy furniture and coarsely textured fabrics.

Keep in mind that dark walls tend to "shrink" space. For smaller rooms, choose light-colored woods; reserve dark woods for larger rooms. If

123

your plan for a small room demands dark wood, use it sparingly—on one wall perhaps. Apply textured paint or wallcovering to the other three walls.

Real brick and stone walls provide wonderful colors and textures, but don't despair if your architect omitted them. *Faux* fieldstones and sliver-thin bricks, designed expressly for purely decorative effects, are available in do-it-yourself kits, complete with mortar. Buy enough for one wall or four; directions are on the box.

Wallpaper was originally a bit of decorative refinement for early plaster and wood walls. But today, it is closely identified with country homes. An ever-increasing assortment of designs, colors, and textures puts the country of your choice at your fingertips. There are floral patterns galore, including crewel and calico from India, folk florals based on Pennsylvania Dutch designs, French-flavored floral stripes, and splashy chintz and cretonne designs straight from an English garden. Other rural-flavored patterns include patchwork, bandanna prints, stylized florals; and snowflake patterns masquerading as geometrics, trellis patterns, multiwidth stripes; and representational motifs such as ships and New England street scenes. Pastoral and pretty toiles are popular. So are scenic papers and murals.

Textured wallcoverings imitate linen, burlap, and denim. Often, they offer a "plus"—scrubbability.

Plain painted walls are too lacking in character for Country-style decorating. But add sand to paint, or buy textured paint in the can, and walls take on a plaster look. It's quicker, easier, and cheaper than other wall materials and can be changed with little effort or expense.

If the landlord discourages textured paint, try stenciling the plain painted wall. Stenciling is easy, authentically "Country," and can be painted over before the next tenant arrives.

Plain painted walls can also gain character with added-on moldings to serve as chair rails or create panel effects. Dadoes and wainscots also perk up the plain wall.

Definite "no-no's" for the Country look are foil and flock papers; slick and shiny, wet-look walls; and hard, bright primary colors used on broad areas. And no wall-to-wall mirrors, please. Instead, use large mirrors in rustic frames to play back the wonders of Country style.

"Getting back to basics" in this "today" vacation house means one-room living. The kitchen is separated from the living-room area by a partial wall covered in horizontal board with a clear, natural finish. Covered in rough-textured plaster, the adjoining wall is painted a pow color. Vertical boards in the living room, below, *carry on the Early American influence, emphasized by the fireplace-and mantel treatment, with the homage-inspiring ancestor portrait.*

The Country way with natural wood can be as casual as a cabin on the beach, or crackling and contemporary. For Country-casual ambiance, panel the walls in horizontal pecky-cypress boards. Long, low lounge furniture plays up the lazy line of the paneling to create a room to lean back and relax in. A contemporary case in point is the bath, opposite, *with redwood lumber creating dramatic diagonal lines like the zigzag of lightning in a summer thunderstorm.*

126

What could be more "Country" than a log cabin? Above, boards have been machined with a convex side to simulate the log-cabin look. Real, or fake, such rustic log-cabin walls beg for such Countrified accessories as the weather vane, baskets, duck decoys, and the schoolhouse clock.

Wood does wonderful things for walls. Opposite, pine paneling in a random-length pattern—knots and all—is used for a dado, topped with gingham-checked wallcover. The same paneling, applied horizontally, covers cabinet bases. Plants plumped into a basket and skillets hung handily on wooden pegs imply a nonchalance which gives rise to the phrase "Country casual."

129

EXTERIOR SIDINGS

Exterior sidings like the reverse board-and-batten paneling in the family room, opposite, by designer Pat McMillan, and the cedar shakes covering one wall in the bedroom, above, are excellent for creating special effects in today's Country casual rooms. Rugged enough for the outdoor duty they were intended for, they add unusual lines and textures to the traditional warmth of wood indoors.

BRICKS AND
PECKY CYPRESS

Painted pecky-cypress walls are outdoorsy enough to hold their own in the kitchen breakfast area, above, with its quarry-tile floor and plant-laden étagères. Antique bricks paint pictures of snug harbors in these two Country-spiced kitchens, opposite.

133

There's more to "Country" than Cape Cod, as these two rooms prove. Native-stone walls impart a Shenandoah regional flavor to this mountain cottage, above. The effect is underscored by the reed-and-twig chairs and the tree-trunk table. The Southwest makes its contribution in the room designed by Pat McMillan, at left, with a printed carpet inspired by a Navaho rug. A star motif, lifted from the carpet and interpreted in nails on aluminum panels, becomes the room's focal point. Thin-slat blinds over the sliding glass door shield the room from the desert sun.

The English are famous for their country houses—filled inside and out with flowers. A floral-stripe wallcovering and co-ordinating fabric on bed and at the window re-create the feeling of the English country house—forerunner of today's "garden room." Floral sheets carry out the same theme. And it's easy as pie to shirr them on small rods around the walls.

137

138   *Inscrutably "Country"? Weathered-cedar paneling forms an unexpected background for rattan chairs and a tablecloth of patchwork with strangely Oriental overtones in this room by Edmund Motyka, A.S.I.D. Wooden shutters at the curtainless windows and a woven wicker animal on the table hint at "Country" in foreign places. Strictly Occidental is the room by designer Abby Darer, A.S.I.D., at right, where the walls are in bloom year round. The same flowers are strewn on a matching fabric that covers furniture, tablecloth, and windows in a one-pattern plan that makes color scheming a breeze.*

A striped wallcovering, color-co-ordinated with the hugh floral above it, creates a dado capped with a chair-rail molding, top. Above, a variation on the dado theme features a painted dado capped with chair-rail molding and a floral-striped wallcovering.

A wainscot painted a sparkling country-morning white is topped by painted walls, top. Botanical prints play up the country garden statement made by the floral gingham slipcovers in an interior by designer Bobbi Stuart. Walls wrapped in paneling with French provincial carvings prove that Country can also be dignified. Floral prints soften, brighten, and lighten the mood created by designer Paul Krauss.

141

A floral-patterned wallcovering in neutral colors is a nod to today's demand for earth tones. Papered floor-to-ceiling, the walls, opposite, get extra impact from homemade, dark wood hollow "beams." A timeless pictorial printed wallcovering with typical kitchen motifs, above, offers a traditional wall treatment that's admittedly quaint, providing pattern aplenty to cozy up the cottagey kitchen.

Fireplaces— Country Warmth

Since ages past, fireplaces have meant good things—warmth on a wintry evening, hot and nourishing meals for early settlers who cooked in big iron pots over the open flames, and hours of convivial conversation and storytelling. Fireplaces are emotionally important in modern homes, even though they serve essentially as a decorative element. Many a dull room is made more interesting by the addition of a fireplace. If it's too impractical or expensive to install a traditional fireplace, there are artificial fireplaces that look convincingly like the traditional, woodburning variety. Freestanding stoves offer other charming alternatives. They can usually be installed with minimum expense and effort, to become effective decorative focal points with all the convivial flavor of a country store. There are authentic recreations of many old-fashioned stoves. Some of these stoves require zero clearance, which means they can be installed near the wall or directly on the floor. (Be sure to check your local ordinance.) In addition to their good old-fashioned looks, woodburning stoves take a big bite out of your fuel costs. Some models promise to burn several hours on a single log.

Fireplaces are natural focal points and it is usually easy to group furniture around them. In the winter, of course, the wood is always laid. In the summer, take a tip from homemakers of the past and place a pretty firescreen in front of the chimney. Or, bank the fireplace with potted green plants (with a grow light, if necessary) instead of logs.

144

In our earliest country houses, fireplaces were vital for cooking and heating. They were often large enough to walk inside, like this one. Besides offering physical warmth, they provided psychological comfort from the harshness of that early existence. And that's still true today.

146
The hearth and ceiling-high chimney breast of the fireplace, in this den near Memphis, are faced in a massive regional stone. Attention-getting black mortar accentuates the stone and dramatizes the fireplace. A heavy plank mantel rests on two supporting brackets embedded in the stone. Designed by Patricia Hart McMillan. Below, light brick faces the wall, fireplace breast, and built-in wood-box in this garage-cum-garden-room/den by Abby Darer, A.S.I.D.

Old brick, facing hearth and chimney breast, lends Country influence to modern architecture in the living room above. The simple, straight lines of the fireplace repeat the attitude of the walls and ceiling. A matching beam, embedded in the brick, serves as a mantel under the carriage lamps that shed light on this interesing fireplace focal point.

147

Above left, *a knotty-pine wall and mantel, both treated to decorative moldings, are plainly unpretentious and delightfully informal.*

Above right, *a wide swath of brick, applied floor-to-ceiling, calls attention to a small, plain fireplace in Richard Dillon's carriage house "great room." The mantel shelf runs assymetrically across the fireplace and one side of the wall.*

Below left, *the arched fireplace opening, outlined in brick; wide-board surround, treated to a stenciled "bouquet"; and narrow shelf mantel are all part of this ruggedly individual fireplace design.*

Especially in older, random-built houses, fireplaces are not always beautifully centered on a wall. Sometimes they end up in corners, quaint niches, or other places where upholstered seating pieces just can't congregate. Two lightweight, easy-to pull-up chairs, like these Windsors, and a small tavern, tea, or coffee table make it possible to enjoy sitting before even such an impractically placed fire. Interior design by Margot Gunther, A.S.I.D.

149

STUCCOS

There's something especially provincial and slightly romantic about fireplaces finished in rough plaster. Here are three, each unique. This one, above, features a recessed, arched niche above a simple opening. Its unusual shape and rough surface contrast pleasantly with the gleaming tile flooring. The niche fireplace, top right, features a raised hearth and interesting, conical chimney. The raised fireplace with arched opening, below right, seems especially at home in its desert setting.

Stoves or freestanding fireplaces are both decorative and functional and can be installed in fireplaceless rooms with a minimal amount of fuss. Not necessarily a substitute for a "built in" fireplace, there is a great variety of styles from which to choose—iron, copper-clad, and enameled in a rainbow of colors. Each style makes its own special contribution to an overall design concept, so take your time and select the one that best sets the mood for you. A practical point: Fire codes governing the installation of freestanding fireplaces differ from locality to locality, so look before you light.

153

Not all brick-faced fireplaces look alike. The two fanciful designs here prove that there's plenty of room for imagination. If a little extra storage is needed, build it into the fireplace, like the surely for-show one, opposite, or set plants, bottles, and "things" on staggered steps, like those of the fireplace in Richard Dillon's carriage house, above, which boasts a built-in oven. A niche provides neat and convenient storage for extra logs. And, once summer has come, the fireplace opening may prove just the place for the kitty's bed.

Fabrics— Country by the Yard

Fabrics are a rich source of pattern and color for Country-flavored rooms. They add warmth to wood, soften the hard-edge lines of walls and windows, and delight the eye while doing it all. In the good old days, folks mixed patterns with what may seem like gay abandon to us today. But the reason is simple. Decorating was seldom preplanned: Furnishings were simply added one at a time over a period of years, and old things were complemented, not discarded in favor of the new. The prosperous gave up the practice, but long past the turn of this century, frugal countryfolk continued to braid rugs, piece patchwork quilts, and find all sorts of ingenious ways to recycle every precious scrap of homemade fabric. It's this seemingly unstudied mix of fabrics that especially say "Country" to us today.

Unstudied as some of the early mixes may seem, the ones which impress us most were put together with a knowing eye, for there were and still are good guidelines to successfully mixing and matching patterns. One of the easiest to remember is "Birds of a feather flock together." Interpreted loosely, that means things with something in common relate well.

In the world of fabrics, for example, those with similar background colors usually get along happily. While some colors in the pattern may vary, some dominant ones should be shared.

Similar textures are also apt to go together. Rough, dull, and coarse textures mingle cheerfully; and they are informal and right for Country's

Pattern, pattern everywhere seems to be the hallmark of Country-style decorating. A plethora of plaids, patchworks, paisleys, flame stitches, florals, and geometrics gather gleefully in this country living room. The more the merrier—if yours is a knowing eye.

Bandanna prints, once at home on the range, now are at home in any informal setting. Gingham checks, which came to the New World hidden on the undersides of upholstered French chairs, quickly found their place in the decorating sun. They add a picnic-all-year-round feeling to any room. Small, allover geometric prints once graced New England homes. Now they carry on the New England tradition wherever they're used.

playful ways. They should not be mixed with smooth, shiny, city-slick, too-formal textures. Strong textural contrasts, while intriguing, are too deliberately dramatic. They shout "City," and should be left there.

Patterns should relate in scale to one another and to the room in which they're used. When several patterns are mixed, one should be larger in scale and dominate—be the star. Small-scale patterns are traditionally provincial and right for small rooms. For larger rooms, there are large-scaled floral chintzes, cretonnes, and crewel patterns.

If you're unadventurous, today's fabric market offers an abundance of designer-created co-ordinated fabrics that offer well-planned unity, plus a variety of patterns, colors, textures, and scales that all work together. Even in amateur hands, these preplanned co-ordinates provide foolproof results. Such designs are available in both natural cotton, wool and linen fibers, and in fabrics created by today's technology to look like Mother Nature's originals and act like modern miracles, maintenance-wise. We've come a giant step away from the spinning wheel and handloom. Country-flavored fabrics are so abundant, so obliging, sew-it-yourselfers can stitch up the right Country look for all seasons.

159

160

Small-scale floral prints and windowpane checks in cotton or linen say "Country" in a big way. Alone or together, they create character and color, like the combination of checks and flowers that gives up-to-the-moment drama to the living room, top left, by designer Shirley Regendahl. Flowered dropcloths over checked table skirts add a fillip of freshness to the dining room, bottom left. The deep flounce on the to-the-floor cloth, above, *puts a little bounce into an otherwise sedate room, by designer Peg Walker.*

161

162   Today's designer sheets are a home decorator's delight. Their broad, seamless widths lend themselves to an endless number of relatively inexpensive decorative uses. Here, quilted, they form practical and pretty slipcovers. The green-grass design of the sheets-cum-slipcovers inspires the trellis-and-butterflies design stenciled on a canvas screen and across the window shades. A recycled treasure from true country days and too handsome to keep undercover, an antique patchwork quilt now becomes a bedspread. Interior design by Patricia Corbin.

Country decorating shies away from a too-matched look. Self-conscious fabric co-ordination is a little too slick for the nonchalant look you're after. Don't be afraid to mix a medley of color-related patterns like those used by designer Shirley Regendahl in the bedroom, below, or positive and negative prints of the same pattern, like that at the top of page 160 . . . or even florals and geometrics, like the quilt and ginghams on the bed and window seat in an attic bedroom, above, designed by Abby Darer.

163

THE CASE FOR CALICO

Calico with its galaxy of tiny flowers is unendingly charming and inevitably Country. Since its introduction here, back when the American colonies were fledglings, each year has brought a number of new designs to delight the calico lover. There's bound to be one to please you. Once a pattern reserved for fabrics, now it's possible to cover walls and even floors in materials printed in a cheerful calico. Room, below, by Ann Heller, A.S.I.D.

Calico and patchwork team up to swath a bedroom in green and gold, designed by Shirley Regendahl. Used on ceiling, walls, windows, table, and bed, calico spreads its homey good cheer nearly everywhere—even the ceramic kitty gets a calico cushion.

Haitian cotton, a latecomer to the Country scene, makes itself at home in a latter-day Early American environment, left. Just as adroitly, a calico-like cotton covers sofa and love seat, bottom, to convert a city place to Country ways.

One powerfully patterned fabric—overscaled and dynamically colored—
dominates the "great room," above, where the David Websters live and dine in
their North Carolina Country home. The hugh patchwork design in vivid pump-
kin and violet shows up at the windows as pinch-pleated draperies hung on   167
wooden rings and poles. French doors wear the same pattern, laminated on window shades with matching valances. Quilted, it's upholstered on sofa and love
seat and finally turns up at the table as chairpads and napkins. Designer Patricia
Hart McMillan uses two sympathetic wallcoverings on walls and inside the armoire to provide the pattern mix so vital to the country look.

Bowers of flowers from the yard and by the yard—sprigs, sprays, and bouquets—small, medium, large, and giant-sized—maintain a romantic Country-summer mood all year long.

CHILDREN'S ROOMS

Ginghams, florals, and calicoes are oblivious to age barriers. Equally at ease with adults or children, these whimsical designs create moods that inspire the child in us all. In the little girls' room, top left, gingham checks on bedspreads are treated to Farmer and Mrs. Brown appliqués. A co-ordinating check covers walls and windows. Large-scale gingham and a floral fabric and wallcovering mingle with wicker and ruffles, bottom left. Unsure about mixing patterns? A minifloral, above, used everywhere but the floor, eliminates mixing and emphasizes matching.

171

Architecture speaks, but accessories have the final say! Not every room can have small rustic windows and Dutch doors, but each can have accessories that underscore its Country character. Take a tip from this interior whose open-door, you-all-come Country look is restated in accents of pewter, tin, dark woods, pottery, brass, and old glass. The horse-and-hunt picture and the schoolhouse clock are Country touches—so is the picked-from-a-tree walking "stick."

Accessories— Bits and Pieces of Country

Country-style decorating is a sort of visual "ode to everyday," and the focus is on the uncommon beauty of common, everyday objects. Beauty is definitely in the eye of the beholder, and about the only rule in accessorizing the Country room is to eschew the too-fine and avoid the formal like the plague. As a guide—when in doubt, choose pottery *not* porcelain, pewter *not* silver, cotton *not* crepe de Chine.

Relaxed, easygoing Country interiors take kindly to recycled trash-turned-treasure and found-objects-become-*finds*. These live-and-let-live rooms give equal time to backyard botanicals—hollyhocks, zinnias, and sweetpeas—and backroads bounty—Queen Anne's Lace, wild carrot, and all weeds *cum* flowers. Country rooms make way for collections of all sorts—wooden toys, soldiers, spoons, cutting boards, candlesticks. . . . A passel of pretty pillows piled high in a corner, on a daybed, or in a bay window are welcome. So is a handful of glass marbles in bottle or bowl and penny candies or colorful beans and lentils in glass canisters. Tin tubs turned into log holders are fine by the fireplace. Tin painter's buckets may collect overtime as containers for bouquets. Farmers' tools, long since absent from the fields, can add a certain *nostalgie de la boue* to living room, family room, and kitchen walls. Baskets, of course, abound in country interiors. Hang them from beams, in a composition" on the wall, from S-hooks on a ceiling-hung chain, or around the frame of an uncurtained window. Use them as *cachepots*; as containers for nuts, bread, fruit, popcorn, or crackers; as wastebaskets; or to hold logs, magazines, newspapers, or your knitting. There are countless ways to show and use all kind of baskets.

173

Accessories that please the eye, add fragrance to the air, and generally delight the senses pose prettily inside an antique bonnet case dressed for the occasion with dc-Fix *self-adhering vinyl wallcovering in a provincial pattern.*

COUNTRY CLOSE-UPS

Flowers, fresh from the garden and plopped in a favorite basket, are natural Country. So are hurricane lamps with glass globes, miniature toys, and duck decoys . . . Country, naturally. A collection of candlesticks, milk-can lamps, and schoolhouse clocks . . . naturally Country.

OUTDOORSY

*Plants and wicker are almost
as Country as ham and eggs.*

A controlled clutter of useful items comfortably at hand contributes to a casual air and accessorizes this live-in room. A window on the world outside is unfettered, save for the fringed window shade which reveals the view at the flick of a wrist.

LET IT ALL HANG OUT

The Country way with kitchen tools and treasures is to let them all hang out—in full view—where "pretty but useless" and "pathetic but useful" are given equal time.

In designer Larry Peabody's Country kitchen—hanging baskets are a novel and nice window treatment . . . plates on an open shelf provide a feast for the eye . . . and the heavily laden table explains the origin of the term "groaning board."

HANGING ACCESSORIES

Walls are for hanging favorite pictures (in the narrow space between counter and cabinet—protected by glass, of course), clocks, and groups of baskets.

A *harvest* of *pictures*—prints or portraits, landscapes or still lifes—is especially satisfying. Don't hesitate to switch them around from time to time for a fresh look at old favorites.

COUNTRY CLUTTER CONTAINED

The most comfortable clutter is that which is seen and not stumbled over. Open shelving helps to keep a tight rein on objects which might otherwise roam, and it can be a build-it-yourself project, like that in this kitchen.

Man shall not live by bread alone, as this baker's rack demonstrates. . . . There's also bric-a-brac of all sorts.

Shelving can also be salvaged rabbit warrens like these, above, or a bona fide hutch like this one, below.

COMFORTABLE CLUTTER

Top, *choose accessories for the kitchen as carefully as you would those for other rooms. If the furniture says "Country French," the accessories ought to speak the same language. Furniture and accessories agree upon an Early American theme for this family room, above left. Only the Queen Anne chair favors formality, but it's outvoted by the democratic gathering. A pile of pillows proves a Country point in a bedroom, above right, all fitted out with fern-patterned paper.*

The chunky candle, tucked in a newel post and surrounded by silk flowers, is a simple, Country way of saying, "Hello, we're glad to see you" or "Good-by, we're glad you came!"

186   *Stencil painting is an Early American craft now riding high on the tide of nostalgia. And no wonder, when it's updated and fresh as these room fashions, above. The charming window shade came home from the store in boring white. The presto-chango magic comes from a stencil kit and acrylic colors. Flowerpots, wall border, and even the stenciled chair pillows all sprang from the same easy source. Turn the page and see how it's done.*

Countrified Handcrafts for Your Own Home

The handcrafted look is the essence of Country. Handwoven, hardcarved, homespun, handmade . . . it's the touch of human *hands* that warms the wood, clay, and flax, that softens it to our eyes and reaches our sense of continuity, of tradition. Hard-edged is out. Machine-made is offensive. We seek to touch base with our basics by laying hands on our homes. This chapter is here to tell you how to . . . how to pick up the handcrafts our forebears lay down a generation or so ago and how to use them to shape our natural habitats to reflect personal, important values.

We are *not* going to turn you into potters, basketweavers, or macramé artists, although their creations fit naturally into Country rooms. Here, we're into the handcrafts that came as a natural adjunct to Country homemaking: sewing, painting, rugmaking, and such. These were essential skills in those days when doing-it-yourself was the only way of life, not a weekend avocation. Now, of course, doing-it-yourself has all those added emotional qualities: we can satisfy our souls, our sense of self-reliance, and baby the budget in the bargain.

187

STENCILING— ARTISTRY FOR THE UNARTISTIC

For a handcraft that began as an imitation of something else, stenciling has certainly come into its artistic own. Back in early America, the poorer colonists used stenciled designs to simulate the imported wallpapers their better-to-do neighbors could afford for their homes. Although there's evidence that even the Egyptians resorted to stenciling their hieroglyphics, it was these Early American imitators of wallpapers and also of rugs that preserved stenciling through the years until its renaissance in the late twentieth century.

Today, the art has leaped off the wall and onto other home furnishings: furniture, windowshades, and fabrics. Anything, in fact, can be stenciled, thanks in large part to modern acrylic paints that work on almost every surface.

Stencil designs are easy to come by: You can draw your own and cut it from stencil paper (available at any art store); you can buy books already printed with cut-and-use stencil designs, or, easiest, you can buy complete stencil kits, with the designs already punched out of clear, reusable plastic. Add a few tubes of the right color acrylic paints and a special short-bristled stencil brush (again, your art supply store is the source); and the project ahead is as much fun as eating peanuts . . . and just as hard to stop.

Unfinished furniture is finished with a flourish of painted-on flowers. Hand-painted furniture is a charming tradition that stretches back into the Country homes of yesteryear. Pennsylvania Dutch work, for example, is world-famous. You can carry on the tradition with stenciling, applied to primed or painted wood, then protected with successive coats of clear lacquer or polyurethane varnish.

Inspiration is where you find it. Above, a machine-made area rug touched off the artistry that makes merry on the cabinets in this cheerful kitchen. The rug's design has been copied, first on tracing paper, then transferred and cut from stencil board. A few flicks of the brush and the stylized flowers burst into bloom on the drawer and door fronts.

Stencil hints: Use masking tape to keep the stencil from slipping while you paint. "Pounce" the brush on newspaper after dipping in paint to avoid overloading the stencil. To paint in the design, hold the brush straight up and down and work from the edges in. Remove stencil carefully so you don't smear.

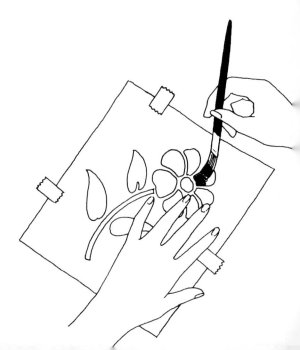

SPATTERPAINTING—
SLAPDASH ART
FOR FLOORS

Spatterpainting is a happy-go-lucky solution to decorating down-trodden floors. The early American settlers discovered it quite by accident, the story goes, when a careless house painter decided to compound his spatters instead of cleaning them up. Well, true or just charming, the story speaks for just how easy spatterpainting is . . . and how much dash and splash it can add to a Country-flavored room.

To spatterpaint a wooden floor (it works equally well on bricks and cement if you use the proper paints—consult your dealer), give it a solid coat of deck enamel and let it dry thoroughly. Now, with masking-tape, attach a protective layer of newspapers all around the lower walls in the room. To apply the paint spatters, you'll need a whisk broom with short stiff bristles, and a stick, ruler, or wooden spoon to stroke on the spatters. Dip just the tips of the bristles in the paint, wipe off till the drips stop, then hold the brush about three feet off the floor and stroke with the stick or spoon to make the droplets fly. The higher you hold the brush, the bigger the spatters will be. If you want to mix spatter colors—the colonists loved this happy confetti look—wait till each set of spatters is dry before adding another.

*Stroking on the spatters
with a wooden spoon—
the higher you hold
the brush, the bigger
the spatters.*

COUNTRY
IS RICH TEXTURES

Texture paint is another product of these good new days that makes it easy for your rooms to look like the good old ones. Satisfyingly thick and creamy, the latex-based paint goes on like any other, using brush or roller, but here the similarity ends and the fun begins. You can attack the wet paint with a notched trowel and swirl it into plasterlike patterns. Or go after it with a crumpled paper towel to produce rough, stuccoesque peaks. Try combing it, literally, for added textural interest, or working it over with a twine-wrapped paint roller. You get the idea. The paint comes in several colors, although white is just right for real Country walls.

1. *Latex-based texture paint goes on with roller or brush, then takes to trowel action for added surface interest.*
2. *A crumbled paper towel, pressed at random into the wet texture paint, produces staccato stucco surfaces.*

191

FURNITURE REFINISHING

Grandma's attic has never been more in style. Anything that's funky, funny, or from another era is well worth climbing the stairs for. Worth rummaging through flea markets and rescuing from street curbs, too. Nostalgia is crowding night-school classes to the doors with people learning the fine points of furniture repair and refinishing, down to the Old World crafts of chair caning and marble-top maintenance.

Here's a short course in reclaiming yesteryear's golden good things for today's Country rooms.

Refinishing. It's really not the horror you've always heard. Refinishing boils down to three basic steps: (1) Remove the old finish if it's in really

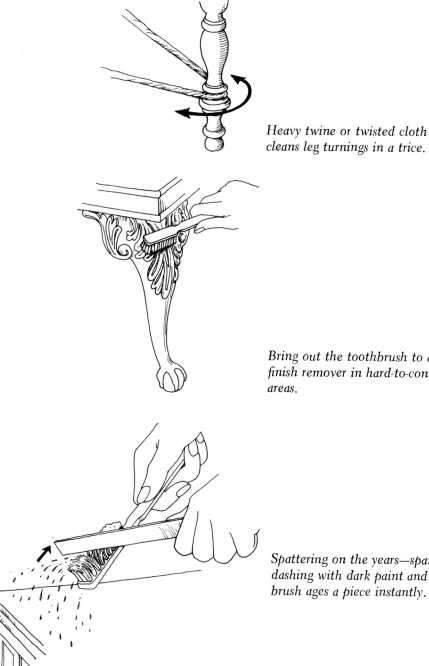

Heavy twine or twisted cloth cleans leg turnings in a trice.

Bring out the toothbrush to apply finish remover in hard-to-conquer areas.

Spattering on the years—spatterdashing with dark paint and a toothbrush ages a piece instantly.

sad shape; (2) Repair and smooth the surface; (3) Apply the new finish: add color stain and protective surfacing of shellac, lacquer, or varnish.

- *Removing the finish.* Investigate the "dip-strip" centers franchised for operation in various parts of the country. You haul the piece there and it's submerged in a tank of remover that melts away the old finish. Dip-stripping is super for pieces you feel fairly casual about, but the process is too harsh for really fine furniture. For stripping at home, arm yourself with a liquid or paste finish remover and follow label directions. Generally, they'll tell you to brush on the removing solution, wait till the surface softens down to the wood, then scrape away the whole gooey mess with a putty knife. On carved areas, use steel wool or a toothbrush. Use heavy string or a twisted fabric strip on table and chair-leg turnings.

Finally, most manufacturers tell you to double-clean the stripped furniture with a solvent. Don't skip this important step or the stain won't go on evenly later.

- *Wipe-staining.* The first step is sanding and sanding and sanding, to make the surface satin-smooth and blemish-free. Use increasingly finer grades of sandpaper, finish with steel wool, then wipe away every trace of sawdust. Spot-test the wiping-stain, say, under a drawer to make sure you like the color, then brush it on and relax. There's no need to fret over grain direction or smooth application. Wait till the wet shine dulls, then go to work with a soft cloth, vigorously wiping away the stain until you like the color you've got left. In twenty-four hours, the piece will be ready for:

- *Finishing.* This is the final, protective coating that is brushed over the dry, stained surface. Shellac is easy but a bit overshiny for the Country look; lacquer dries extremely fast (not always an advantage), so varnish is the most popular finish. Available in both glossy and satin surfaces, it is tough and resistant to water and heat. The traditional type takes forever to dry, so opt instead for polyurethane varnish that sets up tough and fast.

- *Antiquing.* This is instant aging in a can. Instead of waiting years for furniture to take on the patina we cherish, paint it on out of a kit or, cheaper, make up your own combination of glazes to go over the basic coat of semigloss enamel. The steps are similar and simple: Let the base-paint coat dry, brush on the glaze colors, and wipe off till you like the looks of what's left. Spatterdashing, spattering small dark dots of color on the surface, also adds instant age. Use a toothbrush, dark brown paint, and a pencil or stick to stroke on the spots. Spatterdashing is usually done *over* the base paint and *under* the glaze; make sure your glaze won't smear the spots.

IN CASUAL COUNTRY CAFES ARE SEW SIMPLE

Cafes are easy-does-it window wear for Country rooms, simple to sew, to hang, and to live happily with. In single or double layers, they can go to any length to suit your room—from the top to the sill or floor, from the half-way point to the sill or floor, or from the sill itself to the floor, creating the nice illusion that there's more to the window than meets the eye.

To make your own, install the hardware first, then take your measurements for fabric. Measure from the rod or from the cafe rings to the point where the hem will fall and add up to six inches for a double hem. The extra allowance at the top will depend on how the cafes are to be finished; for example, pleater tape calls for a tiny half inch extra; gathering requires four inches extra; the allowance for scalloping depends on how deep the scallops are. To figure the *width* of the fabric you'll need, measure the window area to be covered, double for fullness (triple with sheers), and add at least six inches for double side hems on each panel.

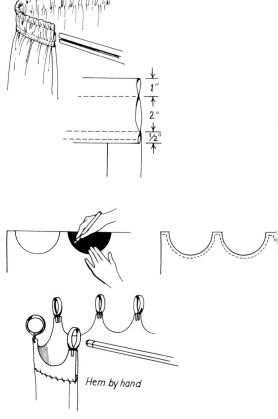

To make a jaunty gathered heading for cafes or for full-length curtains, make side hems first, then turn the top of the fabric to the back 4 inches (more if you want a fluffier heading). Turn the raw edge under ½ inch and stitch across 1 inch from the top, then 2 inches below that as shown. Gather on the rod.

A scalloped heading adds character to short cafes in an informal window scene. Decide how deep the scallops will be, then cut a pattern from folded brown paper (a saucer comes in handy here). Fold the top of the fabric to the right side at least 1½ inches deeper than the scallops, and pin to hold. Now trace your pattern, leaving 1 inch between scallops, and cut out. Stitch around scallops. Unpin bottom edge and turn scallops rightside out across the top. Turn under raw edges at top and sides and hem top by hand as shown. With clip-on rings, the cafes are ready to hang in a flash.

Hem by hand

Jaunty cafes casually gathered on spring-tension rods add the extra punch of color this small sunroom was crying for. And when the shades are raised, the curtains are still on duty, guarding the privacy of the room's occupants.

FABRICATE
A COUNTRY WALL

There's every good reason for fabric-covered walls to be in fashion. First, they've always been handsome, adding a dimension of visual warmth beyond that of most other wallcoverings. But, most important, fabric-wrapped walls add a dimension of actual warmth. They're energy-efficient, decorative draught-dodgers, super sound-absorbers. And, they're no more expensive or difficult to put up, no more trouble to keep clean than other wall-coverings, thanks to wide-width fabrics that refuse to wrinkle or absorb soil (especially sheets, where a king-size yields the equal of 8¾ yards of 36-inch-wide fabric).

There are several approaches to the fabricked wall. You can shirr it up, on small round rods, or use a staple gun and lay in the gathers by hand as you go. That's easiest *if* your wall will hold the staples and *if* you don't mind leaving a few holes behind. Negative on either count? Then you'll have to frame off the area to be fabricked with narrow furring strips, nailed at ceiling and floor lines and all around windows and doors. The fabric itself is then stapled to the furring frame.

Hanging the fabric in flat panels saves both yardage and aggravation, especially if you feel free to apply it directly to the wall. All you need is a good vinyl-wallcovering paste. Spread it on the wall and press on the fabric, turning under top and bottom an inch or so and butting edges carefully. (About those edges: You can turn them under slightly and glue. Or overlap selvage-upon-selvage when you apply the next fabric panel; then go back with a razor and metal straightedge and trim through both selvages in one fell swipe to produce a perfectly aligned edge.)

Finally—and easiest—you can use a combination of staples and glue to hang the fabric in flat panels on the wall. You'll also need upholsterer's tacking strips, narrow strips of light cardboard that will keep your joining seams straight. (Buy it from your neighborhood upholsterer or from upholstery supply shops—check the phone book.) Here, just a thin line of glue is needed to hold edges flat; the staples do the real work, and in jig time.

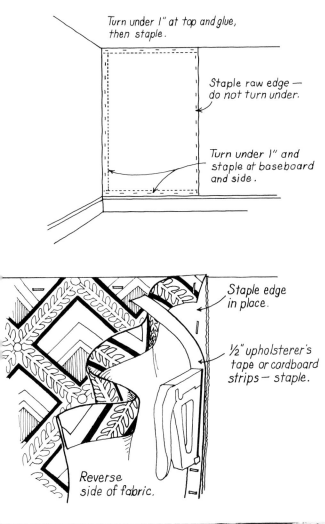

Turn under 1" at top and glue, then staple.

Staple raw edge — do not turn under.

Turn under 1" and staple at baseboard and side.

Staple edge in place.

½" upholsterer's tape or cardboard strips — staple.

Reverse side of fabric.

1. Working from a corner, turn under corner edge and top edge of fabric and run a bead of white household glue across ceiling line. Staple across top edge. Pull bottom edge taut to baseboard and staple. Staple down turned-under edge in corner, then staple down the other vertical edge, smoothing fabric as you go.

2. To hang second panel of fabric, place it, right side down, along the outside edge of the first panel and staple lightly to hold. Now run upholsterer's tape over both edges and staple securely all the way down. Pull the top panel back over the tape to the uncovered side of the wall so the right side is now out and the joining seam is smooth. Turn under top and bottom edges and staple down vertical edge as before. Successive panels go up the same way.

Allover brightly—J. P. Stevens' crisp blue-and-white sheets put sparkle in designer Marlene Siff's own Connecticut bedroom. Applied flat to the wall, sheets are topped with a valance that runs completely around the room and over the windows, too.

BRAIDED RAG RUGS

If *you* had to cultivate a crop of cotton, pick and gin it, then card and spin and color, before finally weaving it into cloth, you wouldn't be eager to toss that fabric away after it was outgrown, either.

That's why country women invented rag rugs. They offered one more way to urge the last remnants of use from every scrap of the fabrics our foremothers struggled so to make. Frugality, not fashion, was foremost in their minds, but the resulting floor fabrics took on a kind of helter-skelter, confetti-colored status of their own. It's a look that's right underfoot in casual Country rooms today, and it's just as budget-loving now as it was then.

Only time and a good collection of scrap fabrics are required to make

Round and round the rug goes, adding a kind of insouciant charm to the floor of this Country collector's family room. Back in the old days, the fabric braided into such rugs had gone round and round, too, from closet to floorcovering, till every bit of use had been wrested from it.

your own braided rag rug. Skills can be minimal: If you can braid your daughter's pigtails and thread a needle, you're set.

To get ready: Put all the old clothes you can come by in a pile. Cut off zippers, buttons, collars, cuffs, pockets, and waistbands. Let out the seams so that everything's flat. Now follow the fabric grain to cut the fabrics in strips approximately 1¾ inches wide and as long as possible.

Now move to your sewing machine. With right sides touching, stitch the strips end to end so the fabric grain is on the bias. For a regular oval rug, make them as long as possible. For a rug made of individual rounds, sew four-yard lengths. Roll each up, leaving a couple of feet hanging out, and snap on a rubber band to hold the balls.

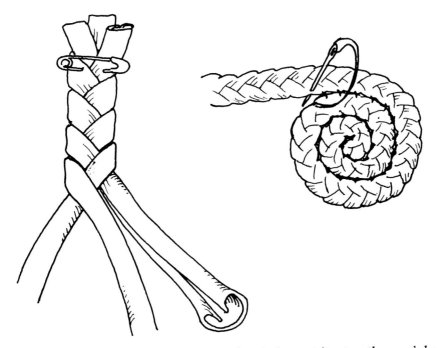

For a traditional braided rug, pin the ends of three strips together and braid snugly, folding the outside edges of each strip to the center to hide raw edges. Start with a center coil and wrap the braided lengths round and round, hand-stitching with strong thread as you go. Tack on additional strips as needed, and when the rug is as big as you want, turn under the edge of the last strip and catch in place by hand.

For a rug made of individual rounds, pin and braid three 4-yard lengths at a time. You'll end up with a braid about 2 yards long. To coil each braid into a round, tuck the top end into a circle and stitch, then coil the entire length, stitching to hold as you go. Tack the loose end, and steam the circle with an iron and a damp towel to make it lie flat.

When you've got enough coils to cover the area you're dressing, arrange them on the floor and stitch securely together where they touch. You may want to make some smaller coils to fill in between the larger. The procedure is the same.

THE MOST GRACEFUL TABLE DRESSING AROUND

The Victorians gave the round tablecloth stature. Typically, it dressed whatever large table stood right smack in the center of the parlor, and upon it were heaped all kinds of memorabilia and keepsakes ("whatnots," as the Victorians knew them).

The round table has long since been let out of its parlor-proper role. Thank goodness. It's one of the most graceful looks around, adding the softness, color and, perhaps, pattern that's so welcome in a roomful of furniture legs. The emphasis, as you've just seen, is on the table cover, not the table itself. For that, any old round will do, including plywood cut to size, mounted on some nondescript support, and padded with fiberfill, or an old sheet or two, stapled on.

A round cloth only looks complicated to make; actually, you simply scissor it out of a square of fabric made to equal the measurement of your table from the floor to the tabletop on both sides, then across the top of the table itself. Add these three figures, plus an inch for the hem, to get the size of the fabric square you'll need to make. The illustration (left) shows you how to join fabric pieces together. (Right) Fold the fabric square in half, pin or tack a tape measure to the exact center, and mark off a half circle equal to *half* the measurement you need. Pin along the line, cut out, and hem. Your cloth's ready for trimming, if you're so inclined.

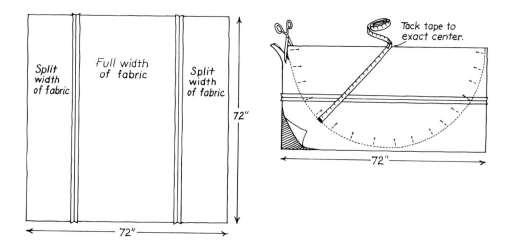

A *round cover is* haute couture *dressing for a small dining table, especially when it sweeps the floor in graceful folds. Practicality has its place, too: You can make a square overthrow to protect the long cloth and provide easy tablescape changes.*

COUNTRY WAYS WITH WALLCOVERINGS

Wallcoverings are the victims of a great cover-up; for entirely too long now the world somehow has covered up the fact that they really are very easy to hang yourself. Easy and rewarding: the work goes quickly—in minutes, you have a bright new look beginning to bloom in your room. Yet the paste sets up slowly, so you can be leisurely about getting everything right before moving on to the next panel. Hanging your own is *not* the mess and mayhem all those jokes about one-armed paper hangers have led you to believe.

1. *Measure from a corner out ½-inch less than the wallcovering's width. At this spot, snap a plumb line. (Use a weighted, chalked string. Tack it at the top and when the weight hangs still, snap the string against the wall.) Cut your first strip of wallcovering as long as the wall is tall, plus an extra inch or two at the top and bottom.*

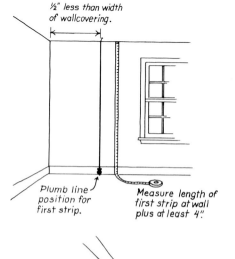

½" less than width of wallcovering.

Plumb line position for first strip.

Measure length of first strip at wall plus at least 4"

2. *Mix paste according to directions. (If you're using prepasted wallcovering, buy a waterbox from your dealer. It's cheap and directions come with it.) Spread paste on back of the first strip, skipping the top inch or so. Fold in thirds as shown, pasted sides touching.*

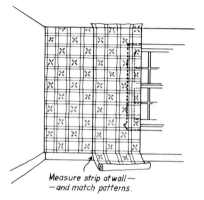

3. *Align first strip with plumb line, then brush smooth onto wall, working from center to edges.*

Measure strip at wall— —and match patterns.

What wallcovering *is*, is a delightful way to build a Country mood from your walls out . . . with rich embossed textures that look like burlap, linen, basketweaves; with fields of flowers; with tattersalls and plaids and tiny provincial prints Since pretty is as pretty does, look for wallcoverings that come pretrimmed and prepasted (just dip and hang) and are easy to strip clean off the walls when you change your mood or your abode.

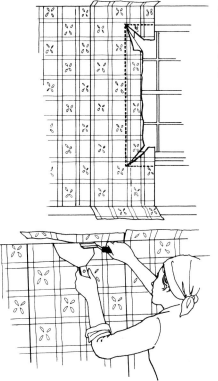

4. *Use razor and straightedge to trim overlap in corner and at top and bottom edges. Bring up the next strip and align with first, matching pattern down the edges, then paste and proceed as before. When you arrive at a window or door, position strip right over it as shown.*

5. *Make rough cuts in part of panel that overlaps window or door, then use razor to trim exactly. When you've hung several strips, go back and use your seam roller to smooth each seam flat to the wall. Wipe off any excess paste you may roll out in the process.*

6. *European way with walls, now available in this country for the first time, is an amusing cross between wallcovering and stencil painting. You actually roll the designs on your wall, using a device that comes with a paint container and interchangeable rollers to give you a choice of patterns.*

203

PANELING FOR COUNTRY WALLS: WOOD YOU BELIEVE . . .

Wood paneling was about the first refinement settlers sought for their homes. First pass, they settled for plain boards, literally the inside view of the outside construction materials. Or, at best, they may have dabbed on plaster, more to cover cracks and ward off draughts than as attempted interior decoration. But with the first hint of leisure time, our forebears went to trimming and planing and even carving wooden panels to warm up their inside walls for the soul's sake now, as well as the body's.

Bless the twentieth century, we can practically bypass the trees and still choose from a rich forest of wood-look panels with the kinds of pluses that make them easy to install, easy to maintain. Especially right for Country rooms, there are rough-sawn boards, wonderfully patined barn woods, gnarled and knotty pines with wormholes and adz marks, even panels carved French-provincial-style, or lookalikes for half-timbered walls. All this background ambiance is available in easy-to-handle 4-by-8-foot sheets you can nail or glue up during an average weekened's work. Here's how:

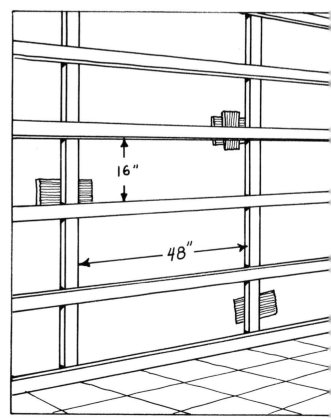

1. Hold a 2-by-4-inch against your walls to see if they're too wavy to glue the panels directly in place. If so, you'll have to frame out the room with a grid of 1-by-2-inch furring strips, spaced as shown and shimmed where necessary. Position the vertical strips so they fall on wall studs (the framing timbers under the plaster or plasterboard coverings, usually placed at 48-inch intervals).

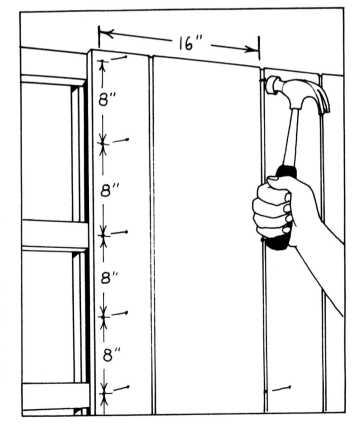

2. *Start installing panels in a corner. If it's uneven, you'll need to use a compass to trace the wall and scribe the first panel as shown. Use a coping saw to cut along the scribed line. Place the first panel against a plumb line (see how on page 202) to make sure it's square; otherwise, all succeeding panels will be crooked, too.*

3. *Glue (following label directions) or nail the panel in place, spacing finishing nails as shown. The outer edges of all panels must fall on a vertical furring strip so they have solid support. Since the same is true around windows, doors, and other openings, be sure to make a furring-strip frame there, too. Your dealer can help select the right stock moldings to finish off the job with a professional flourish.*

The Care and Keeping of Country

MARBLE. The real thing may come as a mystery to generations raised on invulnerable imitations. White or non-yellowing wax will help protect marble tabletops and mantels. Still, any spills should be wiped up immediately to avoid stains—marble is actually porous limestone, and stains sink in readily. When you've got a tough stain on your hands, try ammonia, white vinegar, or a mild detergent, or bleach with a mixture of hydrogen peroxide (the kind you use for hair) and powdered whiting (buy it at paint stores). Make a paste, apply to the stain, and cover with a piece of taped-on plastic wrap so it stays moist while the poultice does its work. Later—it can take up to forty-eight hours—remove the poultice, rinse well, and rub with a marble-polishing compound. Now protect with paste wax so it won't happen all over again.

Etched marks in marble require a special polishing powder, tin oxide, to polish away the damage. It's available from marble dealers and stores that sell marble-care kits. Tin oxide requires a generous amount of elbow grease to be effective, so if you have the kind of buffing pad that's used with an electric drill, bring it into action.

IVORY. Old pianos are getting a replay in this nostalgia-oriented era. If your oldie is *too* golden, you can whiten the ivories with denatured alcohol. Use a soft cloth to wipe it on, then a chamois to polish the keys. If this doesn't do the trick, try bleaching with salt, rubbed in with the juice of a lemon.

CANING. Cane chair seats that have seen better days can be replaced with a length of prewoven cane, provided the seat has a groove around the inside edge fitted with a wooden spline. If your chair seat has holes through which the cane is laced, you'll have to find a professional caner (check your phone directory).

To do the job with the prewoven goods, remove the old spline and save it. If it's beyond reuse, buy a new one from your cane dealer when you pick up the seating. Tack the new length of cane over the open area and use a razor or craft knife to trim all around just outside the spline groove. Soak the spline in water until it's pliable, then put into the groove to check the fit. Trim if necessary, Now remove the spline, run a bead of glue around inside the groove, dampen the ends of the cane, and use a wooden mallet and wooden wedges to drive it down into the groove. Start at the back; leave a wedge in place there, then at the sides, and finally at the front. Don't remove the wedges till the glue dries. Then glue the spline over the groove, using the mallet to smooth in place.

CLEANING. Sometimes your choicest finds need only a good washing to make them socially acceptable in your Country rooms. Try scrubbing with white soap and as little water as you can get by with, then dry thoroughly and immediately to avoid raising the grain.

If this doesn't do a satisfactory job, make a cleaner-conditioner of three parts boiled linseed oil mixed with one part turpentine. Apply with a lint-free cloth and rub in thoroughly. The grime should come off on the cloth. Leave the mixture on to nourish the wood.

Old wicker can be washed, using a mild soap and a well wrung-out cloth. A natural fiber, wicker likes a little moisture, but overwatering causes problems.

VENEERS. Since water-soluble glue was the only thing around when many old furniture pieces were created, any dampness down through the years can cause the veneers to come loose or blister. White polyvinyl glue will take care of the first problem. The second is a little more complicated, but still cope-withable. Slit the blistered spot down the center along the grain, using a razor blade. Now lay a folded dish towel over the blister and hold a moderate iron against it to warm up the wood surface. The heat should soften the old glue and get it working again. If the edges of the slit now overlap, trim carefully with the razor and apply the iron treatment again till the spot is smooth. Then weight overnight with heavy books to keep it that way.

WOUNDED FURNITURE. Gouges and scratches often succumb to the simplest remedy such as rubbing with the meat of a walnut. If that doesn't work, try an ordinary crayon in the nearest color, or use a wax or putty stick (most hardware stores have them).

Dents are no more than wood with all the moisture knocked out. Therefore, to restore the spot, you must replace the moisture. This is easiest with the protective finish removed from the piece. If, however, you're not willing to get into all that, try ironing out the spot: Lay a slightly damp folded towel over the piece and set a moderately warm iron on it for a few minutes at a time. You should be able to coax the dent into disappearing.

Stalking the Country Auction

Why take the retail route to furnishing your Country home, when you can stalk authentic styles at country auctions? They are the obvious places to find genuinely old pieces that hint of fascinating pasts while contributing to a pleasant present. The thrill of discovery, plus the challenge of bidding, makes buying at auction an exciting experience. But if auction-going is new to you, there are some things you should know before the bidding begins.

Look for notices of auctions in newspapers, tacked on bulletin boards at local country grocery stores, or posted at the auction site itself. Some galleries have mailing lists and will be glad to add your name. You'll receive notice of on-site estate sales as well as regularly scheduled gallery auctions.

Along with a partial list of items to be sold, auction notices give the date of auction and hours for viewing. Take advantage of these preauction opportunities and carefully examine those pieces which interest you, for at auction it's *caveat emptor*—buyer beware! Conditions of sale are "as is"—there are no exchanges, no returns, and no refunds. And, unlike furniture stores, auction houses have no service departments. If you discover afterward that a piece you've successfully bid on is damaged, it will be up to you to repair it.

At preauction viewing, make note of the pieces you plan to bid on and decide the highest bid you will offer. Otherwise, in the excitement of heated bidding you may be tempted to offer more than a clear head should be willing to pay.

If you're not able to attend the auction yourself, you may offer a "reserve" or proxy bid, which the gallery will enter for you. If a higher bid is received, you fall out of the competition. But, if your proxy bid tops the highest bid offered at auction, you win the piece.

Unlike city auctions with printed catalogues and set orders of bidding, country auctions are informal, walk-around affairs. Of course, there are certain business procedures. For these, check with the clerk when you first arrive. (Come early to register and find a good seat before the auction begins.) Normally, you register by giving the clerk your name and address, which will be entered next to a number on a roster. The clerk will write this number boldly on a piece of paper, which you can hold up for the auctioneer and the clerk/bookkeeper to see once you've successfully bid on a piece. (One gallery we know uses a felt-tip pen to write numbers on paper plates, which lend a certain *al fresco* atmosphere to the occasion!) This simple means of identification allows the auctioneer to announce at the close of the bidding, "Going, going, gone. Sold to Number ——, for —— dollars"— a boon to the gallery's busy bookkeeper.

At the point of sale, an attendant will bring a sales ticket for you to sign. Generally, at this time you'll be asked to pay a percentage of the purchase price to hold the piece till the close of the auction.

Since country auctions are informal, it's all right to walk around for a closer look at pieces waiting to be auctioned. (Just be mindful that you don't become a part of the "onstage" proceedings!) And, if you can't wait indefinitely for a particular piece, point it out and the attendant will have it brought up early for bidding.

The auctioneer begins the bidding by calling for a certain starting bid. You may offer less, but he has the right to refuse any offer which he thinks is inadequate. Once the bidding is underway, it progresses in increments of $10 or $25 dollars for more expensive pieces and $2.00 to $5.00 for less valuable items. Increments are usually set by the auctioneer.

When you continue to bid in stated increments, it indicates to all that you are doggedly determined to "hang in there." By doubling an increment you may intimidate other bidders sufficiently that they'll stop bidding, but you run the risk of paying more than you might have, had you simply continued to bid conservatively. By cutting an increment in half, you indicate that you're reaching your limit. This is apt to encourage an opponent who may have been thinking of dropping out of the race. All of these are techniques of bidding which you'll learn to use skillfully to your advantage.

Auctions are cash-and-carry events. At the end of the auction, or whenever you decide to leave, you must settle your bill with the clerk/bookkeeper and claim your pieces. Occasionally the gallery will hold large pieces for twenty-four hours while you make arrangements to get them home. Some galleries will deliver large pieces for a fee. (Of course, when the delivery fee is added to the purchase price, a piece may not prove to be such a bargain!)

In some galleries, if you decide before the close of an auction that you've made a mistake, the gallery will put the item back up for bidding. Or, if this cannot be done and you haven't paid an outlandish price, the gallery will resell the item for you at a later auction at the standard 20 to 25 per cent brokerage fee. When this happens, you should be prepared to buy it back should the bidding not reach the figure you think adequate.

All in all, country auctions are usually great fun. In addition to the treasure hunt, there's food and drink and a sense of merriment that's akin to good theater—country-style.

Fun Furniture Is Where You Find It

The exciting eclecticism of Country comes from "found" furniture—furniture with character found here and there, sometimes in surprising places. Almost always castoffs, such furniture is most often found one piece at a time—a chair here, a table there, and so on. Not meant to match anything, it joins any democratic collection, melding to become a part of an unusual whole. Here are some sources for these *finds*—and how to deal with them.

GARAGE SALES vary from neighborhood to neighborhood. In some instances, one family may decide to clean out the attic or basement and will announce the event in the local paper, listing the more glamorous items in hopes of luring eager buyers. Not usually an extensive showing, it only takes a few minutes to pop in for a look.

Occasionally, several families get together to pool trash and treasures for one big sale either seasonally, annually, or once in a lifetime. Since this is a broader collection from which to choose, the hope of finding a real treasure is greater. The chance is strictly potluck, but there's always that potential something to make the effort worthwhile.

A third kind of garage sale occurs when a family moves. This is a promising event, since the urgency to depart encourages speedy bargaining. Run, don't walk!

Some neighbors seem to always be conducting a garage sale. They are probably amateurs turned professional, and the prices will be commensurate with the expertise of the sellers. But still, it's not a bad idea to go have a look.

Whatever the source of the garage sale, watch the papers for an announcement and a list of items to be sold. If something appeals to you in a sale that is supposed to start on say, Saturday, stop by on Friday. Dealers do! So by the time Saturday rolls around, the best buys have been wheeled off. There's very little chance you'll be turned away if you turn up early. But you may have to bargain extra hard, since the sellers know they can hold out for their set prices until the day of the announced sale.

By the way, even though price tags have been neatly attached to each item at a garage sale, don't hestitate to offer less. If you choose a number of items, you have a strong argument for offering less than the collective price. And since the main purpose of the sale is to get rid of the items, the owners will probably be happy to dicker.

GOODWILL, SALVATION ARMY, and other charity outlets are

another source for old and unusual pieces. Furniture donated to them often comes from empty-nesters giving up big old homes and moving into smaller quarters, from estate settlements, and so on. Here, you are more likely to find groups of matching pieces. By the time you see a new shipment, antique dealers will probably have culled truly choice pieces, but interesting and charming items can still be had fairly reasonably. It pays to cultivate the friendship of the people who run these shops. If you're successful, they'll probably be glad to call you when there's a new arrival that they think you will like. This will give you a chance to look over the selection before the general public sees it. Although such charity dealers have become pretty savvy and you're not apt to find any "steals," still, they're good sources for fine old pieces at fair prices.

ESTATE SALES are announced in local newspapers; unhappily, it's usually after professional dealers have been invited to pick and choose. Since *they're* looking for antiques, you probably won't have a chance in that regard. But if you're happy to buy good-looking and useful pieces, then you will want to attend. Go early—the sooner the better. Pieces are likely to be sold quickly, and if you dawdle, there will be little left to excite your interest. Don't hesitate to go by a day ahead of the date announced for the sale. The early bird catches the worm—and the quaint bird's-eye-maple dresser, too!

VILLAGE OR TOWN DUMP AND CITY STREETS used to be fair game for treasure hunting, but, lately, special passes are required to the dump, and city streets are no longer reliable sources. However, if you just happen to find yourself down in the dumps, don't waste time standing on formality—take a look. And city streets are still good sources for such as produce baskets which make interesting wastebaskets, log holders, and magazine "racks." And—the price is right.

SECONDHAND STORES. Oh yes! Whether they're called "Merry-Go-Round," "Secondhand Rose," or some other quaint euphemism, secondhand stores are fertile fields of great "finds." Inflation has hit there, too, but these stores are rewarding places to look for fascinating furniture that's coming 'round once more on fashion's fickle wheel.

Glossary

ACCESSORIES Small elements like lamps, pillows, pictures, plants, et cetera, that add color, character, and individuality to a room.

ANTIMACASSAR Knit, crocheted, or embroidered doily used to cover back and arms of upholstered furniture to prevent soiling.

ANTIQUE According to U. S. Customs law, a work of art at least one hundred years old.

ANTIQUING Finishing an object or treating it in some way to make it look old.

APPLIQUÉ An ornament stitched or applied to another surface.

APRON On furniture, the horizontal board placed at right angles to the underside of the tabletop or beneath the seat.

AREA RUG A smaller than room-size rug used to set off a special area.

ARMOIRE A tall cabinet with doors, originally used in France for storing armor or tools. Commonly used for clothing or linens.

BAIL A metal loop or ring used as a handle and often attached to a backplate.

BALL-AND-CLAW A furniture foot carved like an animal's claw grasping a ball, popularly used in eighteenth-century English furniture.

BALUSTER A vertical spindle support for staircase railings or in furniture.

BANISTER Same as baluster.

BANISTER-BACK CHAIR An American chair of the late seventeenth century, with back uprights made of flat bars or split, turned spindles.

BANQUETTE Upholstered built-in seating.

BERGÈRE French upholstered armchair with closed sides and wide seat.

BLOCK FRONT Furniture with vertically divided front consisting of three panels—a recessed center panel flanked by two raised panels.

BOLSTER A long, narrow cushion—can be round or rectangular.

BREAKFRONT Cabinet with a projecting portion (usually the center).

BROADLOOM Carpet woven on a broad loom in 9-, 12-, or 15-foot widths.

BUN FOOT A support resembling a slightly flattened ball.

BUREAU In America, a chest of drawers. In England or France, a desk or table with drawers.

BURL Veneer cut from irregular growths (such as roots or crotches) of trees, showing beautiful mottled patterns.

BURLAP Coarsely grained fabric made from jute, hemp, or heavy cotton.

BUTTERFLY TABLE A small drop-leaf table; the raised leaf supported by a butterfly-shaped swinging bracket.

CABRIOLE "S" Curved furniture leg; used especially in eighteenth-century French and English furniture.

CAFE CURTAIN Short curtain hung with rings on a rod.

CALICO Plain-weave, coarse cotton cloth, usually printed, originating in Calcutta, India.

CAMELBACK Chair or sofa with a serpentine-curved top rail.

CANE Flexible rattan woven for chair and sofa backs and seats and for cabinet doors.

CANOPY Drapery suspended usually over a bed.

CHAIR RAIL Horizontal molding placed on the wall at the height of a chair back. Sometimes the topmost molding of a dado and called the dado cap.

CHAIR TABLE A chair with a hinged back that can drop to a horizontal position to be used as a tabletop.

CHAISE LONGUE A chair with a very long seat for reclining.

CHEST-ON-CHEST A chest of drawers in two parts, one stacked on top of the other.

CHIFFONIER A tall, narrow chest of drawers.

CHINTZ Cotton fabric, usually printed with large floral patterns, may be glazed or unglazed. Takes its name from a Hindu word for "spotted."

COFFER An ornamental sunken panel in a ceiling.

CRETONNE Heavy cotton material printed with large (usually floral) patterns. Named for Creton, the Norman village where it was developed.

CREWELWORK Embroidery on cotton or linen, usually simple stitches worked in floral designs.

DADO Lower part of the wall treated differently from the top, by use of paneling, paper, etc.

DIAPER PATTERN An all over, repeating pattern without definite limits.

DENIM A heavy cotton in a twill weave. Originally for work clothing, the fabric has become popular for slipcovers, bedspreads, draperies, and tablecloths.

DISTRESSED Furniture scarred and finished to look aged.

DOVETAIL Method of joining boards in furniture making by fitting dovetail-shaped projections on one piece into matching slots on another.

DOWEL Headless pin, usually wood, used to hold two pieces of wood together.

DOWER CHEST A bride's hope chest used for seating and storage.

DRESSER A cabinet with drawers or shelves and usually a mirror.

DROP LID Hinged desk front that falls forward to create a writing surface.

EGG-AND-DART Ornamental carving on molding featuring egglike and dartlike forms.

ÉTAGÈRE Open shelves, used to show off books, bibelots, et cetera.

FAÏENCE Glazed biscuit-ware pottery originally made at Faenza, Italy. Name is now popularly applied to other earthenware.

FIDDLEBACK CHAIR Rush-seated chair of the Queen Anne type with the back splat in a fiddleback or vase shape. Popular in colonial America.

FINIAL Decorative ornament on top of bedposts, lamps, et cetera, in the form of a knob, pineapple, or foliage.

FIRE SCREEN Free-standing screen, sometimes executed in needlework, to shield from heat and sparks from the fireplace.

FLAME STITCH Undulating, multicolored pattern adapted from a traditional Hungarian needlework stitch.

FLOCK WALLPAPER Paper imitating velvet.

FLUTINGS Parallel concave channels or grooves used to ornament columns in architecture or furniture.

FOUR-POSTER Bed with four tall corner posts.

FRACTUR PAINTING Decorative birth and marriage certificates made in the eighteenth and nineteenth centuries by the Pennsylvania (Dutch) Germans.

FRET OR FRETWORK Ornamental latticework in geometric patterns.

213

Gadroon A decorative band of raised oval shapes that is often seen on silver or furniture.

Gallery Small metal or wood railing around the top of a table or cabinet.

Gilt A thin layer of gold on any article.

Gingham Yarn-dyed, plain-weave cotton; usually checked.

Girandole A wall mirror with attached candle brackets.

Gothic Mid-nineteenth-century furniture style based on medieval architecture and borrowing pointed arches and trefoil motifs.

Grass Cloth Wallcovering made of grass or grasslike fibers.

Grille Metal latticework used in bookcase and cabinet doors.

Gros Point Coarse needlepoint stitch used for upholstery.

Hadley Chest An ornately carved Early American chest; usually with feet and one drawer.

Haitian Cotton Thick, loosely twisted yarn woven into heavy, ruglike upholstery fabric.

Harvest Table Long, narrow table with drop leaves and straight legs.

Hex Sign A good-luck sign placed on buildings by the Pennsylvania Germans; often the shape of a circle, enclosing a six-pointed star.

Highboy Tall chest of drawers with an upper chest sitting on a lowboy.

Hitchcock Chair Painted and stenciled wood chair mass-produced in the first half of the nineteenth century by Lambert Hitchcock.

Homespun Coarse and irregular machine-loomed fabrics made to look handmade.

Hooked Rug Rug made by pushing threads or strips of cloth through a canvas backing.

Hutch A chest; usually with open upper shelves and closed doors at the bottom.

Inlay Contrasting wood, metal, ivory, or other material inset flush into the surface for decorative effect.

Jacobean Furniture, usually of heavy oak with bulbous or twisted legs, made during the reign of James I of England.

Jardinière A container for plants; from the French word for garden.

Kas Large Dutch or Pennsylvania German cupboards; usually painted and carved.

Knife Edge Pillow with single seam on its edge, unlike squared or box-edged pillow.

K.D. (Knocked Down) For furniture that is purchased unassembled to be put together by the consumer.

Knotty Pine Pine boards with rough knotholes showing.

Ladder Back Chair back with horizontal back rails.

Lambrequin Decorative frame for window or doorway; usually wood, covered in fabric.

Lit-Clos French for closed bed.

Love Seat Sofa or chair for two.

Marbleizing Painting to give marblelike look to a surface.

Marlborough Leg A heavy, straight furniture leg with a block foot; much used in mid-eighteenth-century English and American furniture.

214

Marquetry Flush decorative inlay of contrasting woods.

MATCHSTICK Material for window shades made up of rows of thin horizontal sticks.

MILLEFLEURS French for "a thousand flowers"—used to describe floral fabric designs.

MISSION Name given to a particularly plain oak furniture produced in the late 1800s in California.

MONOCHROMATIC OR MONOTONE Decoration in a single color.

MOTIF Decorative idea or dominant theme in design.

NEOCLASSIC New interest in classic style and form.

NEST OF TABLES Small tables in graduated sizes which fit under each other for storage.

OJET D'ART French term for small art objects.

ORMOLU Cast-bronze ornament surfaced with gold and applied as an enrichment for furniture.

OTTOMAN A backless, armless, low-cushioned seat, sometimes used as a footstool.

PAISLEY Colorful, elaborately printed fabric originating in Paisley, Scotland.

PAPIER-MÂCHÉ Paper pulp molded into various decorative objects.

PARQUETRY Woodwork laid in geometric forms for flooring and sometimes for furniture.

PARSONS TABLE Simple, squared-off table, sometimes called the T-square table. Developed by Parsons School of Interior Design.

PATCHWORK Work made of pieces of cloth of various colors or shapes sewn together.

PEMBROKE TABLE A small drop-leaf table with a drawer.

PEWTER Originally poor man's silver, pewter is an alloy of tin and lead loved for its attractive dull gray color and texture.

PIECRUST TABLE A small round table with scalloped edge.

PLAID Fabric woven of different color yarns in a crossbar effect.

PORCELAIN A hard, vitreous, nonporous pottery made of kaolin or china clay. Fine translucent ceramic ware was first discovered by the Chinese—hence the name "china."

POLKA DOT A dot or round spot (printed, woven, or embroidered) repeated to form a pattern on a fabric.

PRIMITIVE Simple, unsophisticated designs by artists who have not developed later, more sophisticated principles.

QUARTER ROUND A convex molding with a quarter-circle shape.

QUATREFOIL A stylized four-leaf-clover design.

QUEEN ANNE Style of furniture named for England's queen who reigned from 1702–14; has distinctive cabriole legs.

RATTAN An oriental palm woven into wickerwork furniture.

REPEAT The size of one complete pattern motif on printed fabric.

REPRODUCTION A copy of an earlier style.

ROPE BED A bed with rope laced to the frame to hold the mattress.

ROUNDABOUT CHAIR A chair designed to fit into a corner; has a low back on two adjoining sides of a square seat and has one leg in front, one in back, and one on either side of the seat.

Rush   Stalks woven for chair seats.

Rya Rug   Shag area rugs handwoven in Scandinavia, often with stylized peasant designs.

Sampler   A piece of needlework meant to show a beginner's skill. Often a small piece of linen embroidered with alphabets and primitive patterns.

Sconce   Ornamental wall bracket to hold candles.

Serpentine   Undulating curved front of furniture.

Settee   Lightweight seating, about twice as wide as a chair, sometimes upholstered.

Settle   All-wood bench with high back and solid arms whose seat is sometimes a box with hinged lid.

Slat-back Chair   An Early American chair with wide horizontal ladder rails between the two back uprights.

Sisal   Strawlike fiber often woven into rugs.

Spatterdash   Random splashing in several colors or shades, usually on flooring.

Spool Turning   Continuous turning, shaped like rows of spools, found on bedposts and chair legs.

Stencil   Design made by brushing paint or dye across a cutout pattern.

Stoneware   A heavy, nonporous, opaque pottery.

Stucco   Plaster or cement covering for walls.

Swag   Draped fabric used at the window.

Terra Cotta   A hard-baked pottery usually made of a red-brown clay. It may be colored with paint or glaze.

Toile de Jouy   Popular fabric of linen or cotton printed with pastoral or historical scenes in only one color.

Tester   Canopy of a four-poster bed.

Tole   Painted tin decorative objects; lampshades, boxes, trays.

Tree-of-Life Pattern   A pattern resembling a tree or vine and showing leaves, branches, and flowers. It originated in ancient Assyria but traveled to England and to the American colonies.

Trestle Table   Long, horizontal board placed on supporting uprights at either end and connected by stretcher to form a table.

Trundle Bed   Bed rolled under full-sized bed when not in use.

Valance   Decorative horizontal strip across window top to conceal drapery hardware. (Also, drapery on a canopy bed.)

Velveteen   Cotton velvet; has thick short nap or pile on plain back.

Veneer   Sheets of handsomely grained woods applied over less showy foundation.

Wainscot   Paneling that goes only part way to ceiling.

Wardrobe   Large cupboard for hanging clothes.

Whatnot   Open-shelved stand for showing off bric-a-brac.

Wicker   Furniture woven from willow or other plant fibers.

Windsor Chair   "Stick style" furniture with a bentwood back frame and legs pegged into the seat at a rakish angle.

Wing Chair   High-backed upholstered chair with extending sides or wings.

Country—
Who Makes It

SOURCES OF COUNTRY FURNISHINGS

ALLIED CHEMICAL CORP., 1411 Broadway, New York, NY 10018 (Pages 36, 60)

AMANA REFRIGERATION, Public Relations Department, Amana, Iowa 52204 (Page 77)

AMERICAN DREW, P.O. Box 489, North Wilkesboro, NC 28659 (Pages 116, 167)

AMERICAN OLEAN TILE CO., Lansdale, PA 19446 (Pages 92, 182 bottom)

AMTICO, Amtico Square, Trenton, NJ 08638 (Pages 94, 103)

ARMSTRONG CORK CO., Lancaster, PA 17604 (Pages 44, 46, 61, 79, 81, 85, 93, 114, 117, 119, 135, 154, 172, 174 bottom, 178, 183 bottom, 184 center)

BARCALOUNGER c/o Hayes Williams, 26 Madison Avenue, New York, NY 10016 (Page 116)

BELGIAN LINEN ASSOCIATION, 280 Madison Avenue, New York, NY 10016 (Page 163)

BERVEN CARPET, c/o Allied Chemical Corporation, 1411 Broadway, New York, NY 10018 (Page 38 center)

BIGELOW-SANFORD, INC., P.O. Box 3089, Greenville, SC 29602 (Pages 41, 47, 105, 139, 160 top, 170 bottom)

BLOOMCRAFT, INC., 295 Fifth Avenue, New York, NY 10016 (Pages 19, 159)

BOUSSAC OF FRANCE, 979 Third Avenue, New York, NY 10022 (Page 101)

BRENEMAN, INC., 1133 Sycamore Street, Cincinnati, OH 45210 (Pages 43, 51, 141 top, 115)

BRUNSCHWIG & FILS, INC., 979 Third Avenue, New York, NY 10022 (Page 107)

CALLAWAY AREA RUGS, c/o Milliken and Co., 1 Dallis Street, LaGrange, GA (Pages 52, 74, 148 top, 189)

CALIFORNIA REDWOOD ASSN., 617 Montgomery Street, San Francisco, CA 94111 (Pages 86, 87, 90, 127)

CAREFREE WALLCOVERINGS, P.O. Box 66, Westerly, RI 02891 (Page 141)

CHROMCRAFT CO., Hayes-Williams, 261 Madison Avenue, New York, NY 10016 (Page 130)

CLUSTER SHED, c/o Hayes-Williams, 261 Madison Avenue, New York, NY 10016 (Page 153)

COLLINS & AIKMAN, INC., 210 Madison Avenue, New York, NY 10016 (Pages 54, 163)

Singer Furniture, 880 Johnson Ferry Road, Atlanta, GA 30342 (Page 37)

SK Products, c/o The Siesel Co., 845 Third Avenue, New York, NY 10022 (Pages 45, 165)

Stauffer Chemical Co., Westport, CT 06880 (Pages 21, 78, 107, 120, 170 top, 183 top)

Stencil Magic, 8 West 18th Street, New York, NY 10010 (Page 162)

Stiffel Co., 41 Madison Avenue, New York, NY 10010 (Page 60 bottom)

Thomas Strahan Co., Chelsea, MA 02150 (Pages 45 top, 89, 136)

Stratford Co., c/o Hayes-Williams, 261 Madison Avenue, New York, NY 10016 (Page 134)

Style-Tex, c/o Lis King Public Relations, P.O. Box 503, Mahwah, NJ 07430 (Pages 99 bottom, 140 top, 143, 200)

Sugar Hill Furniture, Lisbon, NH 03585 (Pages 28–29, 41, 42, 160 top)

Sunworthy, c/o Carolyn Fleig, 331 East 52d Street, New York, NY 10022 (Page 88)

Syroco, Syracuse, NY 13201 (Pages 60 top, 152 bottom left)

Thayer Coggin Co., High Point, NC (Page 24)

Thomas Industries, 207 East Broadway, Louisville, KY 40202 (Page 167)

Thomasville Furniture Co., P.O. Box 339, Thomasville, NC 27360 (Page 57)

Tile Council of America, c/o Lis King Public Relations, P.O. Box 503, Mawah, NJ 07430 (Page 62)

Trend Line Furniture, 343 Third Avenue, Hickory, NC 28601 (Pages 68, 128)

Uniroyal, Inc., 1230 Avenue of the Americas, New York, NY 10020 (Page 53)

Wall-Tex, c/o Creamer Dickson Basford, Inc., 1301 Avenue of the Americas, New York, NY 10019 (Pages 88, 110, 118, 119)

Wallcovering Industries Bureau, c/o Lis King Public Relations, P.O. Box 503, Mahwah, NJ 07430 (Page 152 bottom right)

Waverly Co., 58 West 40th Street, New York, NY 10018 (Pages 36, 41, 42, 45, 47, 141 top, 165, 167, 170 top, 170 bottom)

Z-Brick, c/o Zakin & Comerford, 909 Third Avenue, New York, NY (Page 146 bottom)

Index